That's Just the Way It Was

By Donna Kay Schuessler Bean
In Collaboration with
Joyce Carol Schuessler Werden

Top row: Donna, Marvin, Joanne   Bottom row: Edith(mother), Joyce, Arthur (father) circa 1951

Acknowledgments

A special thank you to my sister, Joyce Werden, for all the editing and writing that she did for this book and for inspiring me to write it! I also appreciate the time and effort that my daughter, Diane Bean put into getting this book printed. Thanks to my daughter, DeLana Hubler and my niece, Carolyn Mershon for the many hours they spent proofreading the manuscript. It is thanks to my nephew, Greg Hopton that there is such a beautiful family tree in the appendix. It takes a village!

Copyright©2023 Donna Schuessler Bean
All rights reserved
ISBN: 9798854444651

Table of Contents

<u>Preface</u>

By Donna Kay Schuessler Bean

*"Even though we may all become extinct,
we can still leave our footprints in the sand."* Dr. Seuss

I was happy and a little surprised, when a couple years ago, my younger sister, Joyce, suggested that she help me write my life's story. Although we didn't really grow up together because of our age difference, we have always had a close bond. We were able to maintain, even strengthen that bond over the years, when as a new bride, Joyce moved across the country to make her home in Connecticut, over a thousand miles away from Iowa.

Joyce's birthday card to me this year touched my heart with these words:

Our hearts have grown closer with the passing of time.
Through the ups and downs of life, we've come to
understand what it means to have each other.
Sometimes we talk often.......sometimes not.
It doesn't seem to matter.
The feelings of closeness remain with me
because I know you are always there.
I love you, Sister....What a blessing it is to call you mine!

So here I am at the age of eighty-nine, passing on the story of how I got this far. I want to share my story, not just for my own reflection, but because I think my experiences may offer something to younger folks as they make their way on their own journey. I learned a long time ago that there are two ways to do better in life. One is to figure it out for yourself, and the other is to pay attention to what others have learned, so you don't have to do it "the hard way" like they did!

As I look back at the values I learned as a child, I'm reminded of a story that illustrates the importance of taking responsibility in life, something my parents instilled in me. Don't just wait for someone else to make things better, do something yourself!

THAT'S NOT MY JOB
Author Unknown

This is a story about four people named Everybody, Somebody, Anybody and Nobody. There was an important job to be done and Everybody was sure that Somebody would do it. Anybody could have done it, but Nobody did it. Somebody got angry about that, because it was Everybody's job. Everybody thought Anybody could do it, but Nobody realized that Everybody wouldn't do it. It ended up that Everybody blamed Somebody when Nobody did what Anybody could have done.

My deep connection with children has been a continuing thread throughout my life, and brought me to a career in teaching elementary school. My children, grandchildren, and now, great-grandchildren shine a light inside me. I taught either full time or substitute teaching over 60 years, gaining valuable lessons in life in dealing with children, parents, and coworkers. I learned the importance of listening and learning from others.

Of course, I was not immune to the downsides of life, but I pride myself in trying to see setbacks as opportunities to turn things around. I found that in order to do that, I needed lots of help from "guardian angels" who supported me at various turns in my life. These friends and family members, and even relative strangers, are the folks who believed in me, even when I had stopped believing in myself. And like so many things, it came full circle when I later learned that I had touched other lives, being a "guardian angel" for them.

I hope you enjoy reading my life's story and find something to take away for yourself. I wish you well in your journey, knowing that we each have gifts to offer along our way.

Foreward

By Joyce Carol Schuessler Werden

My father once reflected that his life on a mid-western farm
began with horse drawn wagons, but that he lived to see a
man walk on the moon. I remember being surprised to think
of that and feel some regret now for never recording any of
my now-deceased parents' stories. I feel privileged to have
the opportunity to be working with my sister, Donna, to write
about her life's journey that began in rural Iowa in 1933. As I
am thirteen years Donna's junior, my hope was to capture the
attitudes and life in rural Iowa, spanning the time that began
with the Great Depression of the 1930s and ending with the
recovery years after the Covid Pandemic of 2020-22. The
experiences in this book are Donna's. I provided a framework
for the book, some historical context, and asked lots of
questions to deepen her stories.

Growing up, our mother used to tell us that the success of someone's life is measured by how much it mattered that they were on the planet. She said similar things at different times with different words, but the message was always the same. In order for you to know success in life, you had to act in ways that improved things, that it mattered that you ever existed. She made it clear that success was not dependent upon accumulating lots of money or having a great intellect. You just had to live in a way that made things better. Navigating through the rough times, Donna was often able to turn the biggest challenges into opportunities for herself as well as for so many others.

Donna's presence in the world has indeed made a difference for the better, and I am fortunate to be her sister. Even with the big gap in our ages, Donna is the sibling closest to my age, and has been like a second mother to me. It has been my honor to help her tell her story.

PART 1

The Early Years
1933-1945

"Waste not, want not." Benjamin Franklin

My parents-Edith Emogene Boyle and Arthur Paul Schuessler
on their wedding day in 1928

Chapter 1
The Times

The Great Depression hit the country in 1929, just four years before I was born, a worldwide economic crisis that lasted ten years. As young parents then, my mom, Edith Emogene Boyle (1908-1984), and dad, Arthur Paul Schuessler (1902-1983), were forever impacted. Out of necessity, we had to be very frugal in every way and often did without many things. As a small child, I remember that we quit eating sugar on things so we would have enough sugar for canning the food from our garden for winter.

Recycling was a way of life for us, although we didn't label it recycling. We just did it! Mom made her own cottage cheese and egg noodles. I can still smell her fresh baked bread right out of the oven! She even made her laundry soap using lye. When she did buy bread from the grocery store, she reused the plastic bread wrappers, and so many other things, like reusing gift wrapping paper multiple times. When your socks got a hole, Mom darned them. If your clothes got a worn spot or a rip, Mom put a patch on. That's just the way it was.

Mom and Dad quickly established regular chores for all three of us children, even at a very young age. We grew up with a sense that our lives were dependent on all of us pulling together, instilling in us a strong work ethic. It was a given that all three of us children would do what was expected of us without complaint. In fact, I don't remember ever hearing of a rebellious child then!

Our visual source of world news was mainly from the newsreels that played before movies at the cinema, although the news was often history by the time we saw it. Since we did not have a television until I was a teenager, we got our nightly news from the radio. We learned about local happenings from the occasional letters we received and from our weekly newspaper, *The Lone Tree Reporter.* It came out every Thursday, featuring mostly community happenings. It included weddings and deaths of course, but also little tidbits like "Edith and Arthur Schuessler enjoyed a pleasant evening of Bid Euchre [their card game of choice] at the home of Alta and Ernest Lenz last Friday evening". Makes me chuckle to think of it now!

Unless we saw someone in person, our main way of connecting with folks was through the telephone, a large rectangular wooden box that hung on the wall in our kitchen. It had an earpiece on a cord that was attached to the left side of the box, a ringer crank attached to the right side, and a mouthpiece that protruded out the front. We were on a party line with about five of our neighbors, turning the ringer crank the correct sequence of "longs" and "shorts" in order to call them. All other phone calls required calling the operator with three long turns of the crank, and verbally requesting the name of the person we wished to speak to, whereupon she would connect us to them. Households didn't have a phone number then, but the operator seemed to know everyone just by name!

Keep in mind that every household on our party line could hear the rings coming in for the other five families. Of course, we knew we were only supposed to answer when our sequence of rings came through (short, short, long was ours), but if folks were curious, they could quietly and carefully pick up the earpiece and listen in on other's conversations. That was one way to find out what was going on!

There was only one phone operator that I can remember when I was little. A sweet lady, who let us visit her in the little phone building located in the nearest town of Lone Tree. I recall thinking she must have worked very long hours because the wire of her headset had thinned her hair in a line around her head! Now I wonder, when did she sleep?! Did phone service close down late at night so she could sleep?!

It all worked much like Lily Tomlin's phone operator routine you older folks may remember from TV's "Laugh In" show. There was a narrow room with a bank of phone connectors on one side that lit up when someone wanted to make a phone call, at which point, the operator plugged one end of her headset into that connection and asked, "To whom do you wish to speak?" Whereupon, she would plug the caller's connection into that of the person they wanted to speak to. It was an amazing sight to watch!

This was the telephone that we had in our kitchen for many years

In my growing up years, I never saw a black person, or anyone who didn't look like us. I had never heard of someone being gay, or even knew what the term homosexual meant. I also wasn't aware of any divorce. Another taboo subject was pregnancy outside of marriage, the worst curse a young woman could have! I heard my mother once mention, in hushed whispers, about an unmarried girl that was expecting a child. I'd also never heard of the word abortion.

An occasional hobo was the only transient person I ever saw back then. These "bums", as Mom called them, could be seen walking the country roads. It made me nervous to see a stranger, even from a distance, but mom explained that they had probably hopped a ride on the train going through Lone Tree, in search of a job. I don't remember bums ever coming to our door, but I heard stories that sometimes they asked for food. I don't think there were such things as homeless shelters then, so they did whatever they could to get by.

Women had gotten the vote only about fifteen years before I was born, but folks still followed the accepted norms of society at the time. It was a "Father Knows Best" America back then, where the men worked to support the family, while the women did the cooking, cleaning, laundry, and took care of the children. Of course, a good farm wife pitched in with the often-difficult farm work as well. While it was in many ways "a man's world", my mother had some unconventional ideas for the time about her little girls, guiding us toward our eventual careers in teaching to ensure that we were prepared to manage for ourselves.

The Temperance Movement was going strong in communities across the country at that time. Women, who strongly opposed alcohol's effects on the family and community, played a powerful role in the movement. On January 29, 1919, Congress ratified the 18th Amendment, which prohibited the manufacturing, transportation, and sale of alcohol in the United States. Though she never spoke about Prohibition, Mom made it clear that it was the devil's work to drink alcohol. In our house we made and drank grape juice, but never ever wine!

In 1939 World War II broke out and changed so much about our daily lives. Although many men were called to fight, farmers were needed to feed the country, so Dad stayed at home with us. Women too supported the war effort, some from our area going to work at the Davenport, Iowa, Arsenal. I still have today a ration booklet that each family was given to limit the purchasing of scarce items needed in the war. I remember how we had to tear out a stamp every time we bought such items as sugar, gasoline, and shoes. When our stamps were all used, we had to wait until the next book to buy items again.

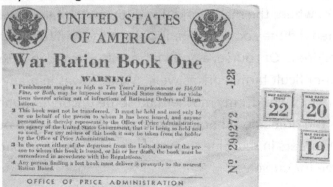

I saved one of our actual War Rations Card and Stamps- They were used to buy gasoline and sugar.

Even livestock feed companies joined the war effort. All of our clothes (except Dad's heavy overalls) were hand sewn by my mother from huge brightly colored cotton sacks that feed for our livestock came in. Mom even made my favorite purple underpants! I had only one Sunday dress. It was also handmade, but amazingly it was not made from a feed sack! It was a chiffon thin material with ruffles on the skirt that stood out when I twirled around. I was always so excited to wear it! All girls/women only wore dresses, never slacks! In winter, we girls wore long stockings held up by a garter belt. They were so uncomfortable around the waist, pulling in all the wrong directions! We also wore long underwear under our dresses to keep warm.

We did not go to stores very often, but when we did, it was to Ross's Dry Goods Store (clothes, fabric, sheets, towels, and such) in Lone Tree. Sometimes we ordered what few things we bought from the Sears or Penney's catalog. Whenever I wanted to buy anything, Dad would invariably ask if I really needed it. If I could justify the purchase, I usually got it, but I learned to think carefully before spending money.

These difficult times taught all of us to be very practical, which served us well for the rest of our lives. Even today, my granddaughters make fun of me for saving the paper and bows every Christmas and birthday! I realize now that my parents had clearly been ahead of their time, recycling and reusing long before it became "the thing to do".

I didn't know of a beauty salon in those days. Mom took care of all haircuts for the family, including mine, my big sister, Joanne's, my older brother, Marvin's, and Dad's. On special occasions, Mom would curl my hair using small rags cut into about one-inch by three-inch strips. She would roll up a small section of my wet hair around the cloth pieces with a knot to hold it. I usually slept on it to let it dry, so I was beautiful in the morning when I combed it out! Other times, she used a hair curling iron that looked like a pair of scissors with rolled edges similar to curling irons today. It had to be heated by placing it in our kerosene lamp shade. When it was hot, it was ready to curl (or singe!) my hair.

Medical care was very different back then. President Roosevelt's New Deal program was the government's first attempt to address the country's health needs. I think that health insurance was available to some in the cities, but not for us farm families. It is no surprise that my parents didn't call the doctor unless we were "at death's door". The polio vaccine and anesthesia for surgery were both in the beginning stages of development.

Mom told me the sad story of how she and Dad had called the doctor for their first child, Maynard Arthur, whom I never knew. He was a month old when he began having difficulty breathing. It was right in the middle of one of our terrible Iowa blizzards, and the doctor couldn't get through to our house to attend to him. It's hard for me to even imagine, but on January 25, 1929, he died in my mother's arms. Mom told us that Maynard died of "double pneumonia".

I realize now that we were incredibly fortunate since rarely was anyone in our family sick. On those occasions when we were, we used home remedies. Whenever we got hurt with a cut or bruise, Mom always made a poultice. She heated broken-up pieces of bread that were soaked in milk. It was very soggy, but not runny, wrapping a cloth around the outside, so that the bread/milk mixture was right on the cut. It worked magically, healing up every wound or infection!

I vividly remember a time when I was about six years old, watching Dad burn some things outside. I decided to play in a huge box nearby when the box tipped over on top of me and landed near the fire. I quickly reached out my arm to right the box, putting it directly into the flames! I had a bad burn on my arm and shoulder that Mom treated with a poultice that stayed on my arm for several days at school.

Imagine living at a time when there was no such thing as an aspirin or an antihistamine. If I had a bad headache, Mom tucked me in bed with a warm, wet washcloth over my eyes and forehead. Traveling salesmen like the Watkins man regularly visited area homes, selling us remedies like liniment or rubbing alcohol. As a child, I had bad leg aches, so Mom would rub my legs with liniment.

When I was very small, perhaps only a toddler, Dad got his hand too close to some moving farm equipment, maybe a combine, and it tore off the end of one of his fingers. I don't know if they called the doctor or if they just attended to the bleeding themselves. Mom told me the story of how it happened when I asked her why one of Dad's fingers was shorter than the others, with just a bit of a fingernail showing at the end.

Mom also told me how, when I was about two years old, I tried to follow her down to the cellar, unbeknownst to her. I lost my balance on the top step and fell off the side of the tall open stairway all the way down onto the cement floor. What an awful scare for Mom who said my nose was bleeding badly and even my eyes were bloody, but I never saw a doctor. Trying to imagine it now, it was a miracle that I lived to adulthood!

Joanne, Marvin and baby Donna in 1934

3
Donna
Aug. 1936

Donna-Age 3

Chapter 2
The Farmstead

The Schuessler farm that I grew up on, as it looked in 1908. The littlest guy in the picture is my dad.

Michael and Mary Schuessler's family in front of the farmhouse they built when they came to the US from Germany. My dad lived there his whole life.

Our farm was located in southeastern Iowa, about four miles from the small town of Lone Tree, population hovering around six-hundred-fifty in 1930. Lone Tree got its name from a giant elm that grew nearby which had served as a prairie landmark for the pioneers going west

To give you the lay of the land, understand that the Iowa Territory had been laid out in squares of six-hundred-forty acres or one square mile, so that after every mile you travel, you come to a crossroad. I remember so vividly that Mom always gave directions to folks using those regular intersections by saying "go four miles east and two miles south". To be sure, the squares were not exactly uniform because of rivers and the natural curvature of the earth, but it was and still is difficult to get lost driving in Iowa!

My dad never moved from the house where he was born until he moved to senior housing near the end of his life. I grew up in that same huge Victorian style farmhouse that he and his eleven siblings were raised. It was built in 1885 with very high ceilings and two beautiful stained-glass windows as well as carved designs on all the doors and woodwork. Over all the inside doorways was a transom window, a small glass window that was designed to crank open or shut to help with heating and cooling of the house. It also had two stairways, the front stairway we used routinely, and the back stairway which was elegantly curved and open with a wide banister. Such fun we kids had sliding down it! Since that stairway wasn't used much, it was also the perfect place to set up my paper doll families which I lovingly cut from the Sears catalog.

Many things in the house had been left behind from the days when my dad's parents lived there. There was a free standing old-fashioned victrola on legs with the huge horn coming from it. It had a cabinet that stored records, mostly the thick seventy-eight RPM that Gene Autry recorded. We had to turn a metal crank on the side to make it work. Whenever the music quit playing, we just cranked it up again.

The house, with its loose-fitting windows, was drafty and cold in our frigid Iowa winters. Our coal furnace wasn't very efficient, barely heating our upstairs bedrooms. The first-floor registers provided the only a bit of heat that floated upstairs. It makes me shiver to think of getting dressed upstairs on winter mornings, often with my breath showing, but at the time we didn't think much about it. That's just the way it was.

My sister, Joanne, and I usually shared a bedroom, since it was the norm then for sisters to share a bed. The closets in the bedrooms were tiny, not really large enough to be called one by today's standards, but to have a closet at all was unusual for houses at that time. Of course, we had so few clothes so it all worked out. The guest room at the far end of the hall had a magnificent antique marble top bedroom set (probably left over from Dad's parents), which I didn't fully appreciate until I was much older.

Our brother's room had a freestanding wardrobe instead of a closet, which was common at the time. Marvin's room was at the end of the hall near the top of the main stairway, making it handy for him to play jokes on me when I was coming upstairs to bed at night. Since he usually went upstairs ahead of me, he often laid in wait for me, just out of sight near the top of the stairs so he could jump out and scare me when I came up. I soon learned to expect his "Boo!" each night, but I jumped a mile every time!

The living/dining room was for relaxing and entertaining. Large family dinners were a specialty of Mom's, around the long heavy dining table with its elaborately carved wooden legs. We also had a floor-standing radio that we gathered around to listen to news and weekly shows. I especially looked forward to "The Shadow" every Sunday night with its creaky door opening! I still get a little chill of excitement thinking about it! It was our weekly tradition to have homemade grape juice with popcorn that Mom made, so that listening to the show was a special event!

We always had an upright piano to one side of the living room as music was central to our family life. Dad especially loved to sing his parent's German songs like "Du, du liegst mir im Herzen" and the old hymns like "In the Garden" and "The Old Rugged Cross". Mom determined that both Joanne and I should learn to play the piano. We both took piano lessons from Nettie Lutz, and later from Mrs. Brown who played the piano and pipe organ at church. I liked both of our teachers as they were very patient with me. It was expected that I would practice every day, but if I got frustrated, I would kick the piano as I practiced!

We also had a parlor, really a formal living room, that we seldom used except for company. Since it was an extra room, that was also where my mom would set up her wooden quilt frame that Dad had made for her. It stayed up for weeks at a time and took up almost the whole room! The church women who quilted would often join her, as they went from house to house to sew on each other's quilts. It was tedious hand stitching, but so many hands working together made it go faster and turned it into a social event. At that time, quilts were not made from matching pieces of material from a fabric shop, but rather from left over scraps of material from past sewing projects. Nothing was wasted, not even odd pieces of fabric from worn out clothes. That's what gives old-fashioned quilts their less-than-coordinated, but beautiful, look. The many hours it took to make one make them extremely prized!

Our large kitchen was the hub of the house, with two small rooms off it, one near the front entry, the washroom, that had a pump over a sink since we had no running water. The other little room was used for a pantry that eventually became an indoor bathroom. The door to the stairs leading to our cellar was also off the kitchen. It was a true cellar (not a basement by any stretch!) with a cement floor. When we got electricity and water in 1938, Dad built a shower down there for himself, really just a shower head with a drain in the floor. He also built wooden shelves for our canned food and a wire-top table to store vegetables like potatoes, onions and carrots.

At that time, we had a wringer washing machine in the basement, along with indoor clotheslines draped from the ceiling to hang clothes in wintery or rainy weather. To dry our clothes in good weather, Dad set up a large area outside behind the house with heavy wires attached to wooden poles in a rectangle. There was no such thing as permanent-press fabric back then. All clothes HAD to be ironed after washing them, and it was not a simple process! The top of the iron had a handle that clamped onto the heavy iron bottom. That bottom piece had to be placed on top of the stove to get hot, whereupon, we clamped the two parts together and ironed until it cooled down. When it did, we clamped on another hot iron that was on the stove and put the cold one on the stove to heat up again. What a job!

Old Wringer Washing Machine and Washtub

Just behind the house was a small brick storage shed that we called the smokehouse, although its days of actually smoking meat were long past. Just to the right of the smokehouse was a long narrow sidewalk that led to our outhouse. Our outhouse had two holes and the all-important catalogue whose pages we used before the days of toilet paper. I remember dreading making that long walk, especially in bad weather. At nighttime, we each had a big pot in our bedroom with a lid that Mom emptied for us every morning.

Unlike some city folks during the Depression, we never worried about not having enough to eat because we had our vegetables and livestock. We grew sweet corn, tomatoes, potatoes, green beans, lettuce, carrots, cucumbers, etc. to eat or save by canning or drying. Planting, weeding, and harvesting were part of our regular routine. Our little cherry tree in the front yard provided Mom with cherries for her scrumptious cherry pies!

The larger outbuildings were essential for getting the farm work done. We had a huge, two-story red barn, the upper floor storing bales of hay for the winter, while the bottom floor provided shelter for livestock and a place for milking with about a dozen stalls. Sometimes when I was watching Dad and Marvin milk, they'd tilt a teat my way to give me a squirt! The feral cats knew whenever it was milking time, since Dad always put out some of the fresh milk in an old rusty, misshapen metal bowl in the barn for them. I tried to keep my distance from the cats because I was leery of them, and I didn't like it when they rubbed their bodies against my legs.

When Dad and Marvin finished milking, they carried the milk buckets up to the house, putting some of the milk into the butter churn for buttermilk and making butter. The rest was poured into our shiny metal cream separator, keeping the milk for drinking, but reserving some to make slop for the pigs. The separated cream went into one of those tall metal milk cans with a lid for the "cream man" to collect. He came every day and bought the cream from us.

Old Butter Churns

We also had a tall corn crib, and a few years later, Dad and Marvin built a metal tool shed to store the tractors, and other equipment. In the open field next to the barn was a tall windmill that was needed to fill the watering trough for the livestock, usually cattle, pigs, and occasionally sheep. We also had an old storage shed that served as a garage for our car, with its own gasoline hose. Farmers needed to have gas onsite for the tractors, but it came in handy for filling our car too.

Children, especially boys, were needed to help with the farm work, and so it was the routine that we kids had regular chores. Gathering eggs was one of our regular twice-daily chores. We had a chicken house behind the house where we raised baby chicks and, when they matured, moved them to the barn where we gathered their eggs. That was not exactly my favorite task, as hens would often peck your arms when you reached your hand under the hen to get the eggs!

The most unpleasant and gross part of raising chickens was preparing them to eat! It's difficult for me to even think about now! I dreaded the morning that we went out to the chicken yard. The chickens seemed to sense that something was up because they began squawking and scattered everywhere. Dad used a wire rod with a hook at the end to catch one by its legs. Mom felt its tummy to make sure it did not have an egg inside, meaning it should be spared as a good layer. If this is beginning to bother you, you may want to skip the next paragraph!

We then brought the hapless chicken to our fenced-in yard where Mom chopped off its head with an ax. It then proceeded to jump all around the yard with its head off. I know firsthand what that expression means, "she was running around like a chicken with its head cut off"! Then we filled a bucket of very hot water and, holding it by its legs, dipped the chicken into the bucket to make it easier to pull off all the feathers, which were very wet and stinky! We took it into the house and held it over the stove fire to singe off all of the hair on its body. Then we had to cut the chicken open below its tail and pull out all of its insides to feed the pigs, although we kept the gizzard and the liver to cook with the chicken. I can't begin to describe the stench! After we washed the insides really well, the chicken was ready to cook or can.

When I was a kid, doing farm work made me feel important, almost an honor. So, you can imagine how thrilled I was when Dad asked me to drive an empty wagon from the field into the barnyard, pulled by our team of huge, white horses. It was the end of a hard day of work so Dad thought the horses would be worn out and easy for me to manage. I was so proud that he thought that I could do that! I did very well until we got to the metal barnyard gate. The back wheels caught on the gate and made a loud noise that spooked the horses. As they turned to run, the wagon box tipped off the wheels, dumping me out into a thorn bush! Fortunately, nothing was damaged except my pride, pulling thorns out of my arms! I ran to the house, thinking that I had failed my job, but Dad was not upset with me at all. His only concern was that I was alright! Nevertheless, I was so disappointed in myself!

Besides our milk cows, we usually had a small herd of beef cattle, and sometimes pigs and sheep. Eventually, they would be sent to the Lone Tree meat locker for butchering, but sometimes Dad did it at home. That was one thing Dad didn't let Joanne and me be part of, but I do know that he hung the animal by its back feet from an iron chain attached to a gigantic hook. It makes me cringe to think of it now, but that's just the way things were. Of course, this was in the days before protein powders or iron supplements, so we got our nutrients the only way we knew how, by including meat in our diet. I think we would have many more vegetarians today if they had to butcher their own meat!

Joanne and I took turns herding the milk cows from the pasture to the barn each day, but I got to do it most often. It wasn't difficult for me to do because the cows were used to the routine, but since we kids were always barefoot in warmer weather, I would occasionally feel the unpleasant squish of stepping in a cow pile while out doing my job! Yuck! In fact, we rarely wore shoes except when going away from home or in cold weather. In the summer, the bottoms of my feet were tough as leather from running barefoot on the gravel driveway!

Our farm neighbors were an important part of our lives growing up. Farmers depended upon each other's help, especially at hay baling times when it took many hands to do the work. When the neighbors got together to work like that, Joanne and I helped Mom fix hearty noon meals for all of the men working in the field. In addition, we took sandwiches and drinks out to the field to them midmorning and mid afternoon. If a family took a trip or needed help, neighbors always pitched in to do their chores and other farm work while they were away.

We had a very long gravel lane that led uphill from the road, probably a quarter mile to our house. Mom explained that setting the house far back from the road helped to keep the gravel dust down in the house. I remember sometimes seeing a huge bull snake sunning itself across the width of the lane. They were fairly long snakes, maybe three feet, and much fatter than a garter snake, and although they were harmless, they looked scary. I was so nervous trying to find a way to tip-toe around it and go on my way! A few times, I freaked myself out when I accidentally stepped on a snake as I hurried down the lane barefooted!

The lane could be nearly impassable in the winter with all our Iowa snow. Although we still used horses to do much of the farm work, when I was about six years old, Dad bought a small Allis Chalmers tractor that had a blade on the front of the tractor to clear the snow (sort of!) from the lane. Dad also put up a long wooden snow fence in the field beside the lane, to keep the wind from drifting it shut, but more than once, we had to leave the car on the road and trudge up the long lane to our front door.

Mom loved her many perennial flowers decorating the edges of our yard. I remember hollyhocks, irises, tiger lilies, and peonies, as well as a magnificent huge rosebush that grew in front of the big bay windows of the house. It was covered with yellow miniature roses all summer! So beautiful! For the rest of my life, I determined to always have a rosebush in my yard. It was a summer ritual for Joanne and me to make hollyhock dolls by the dozens! We also had a row of fragrant lilac bushes (swarming with bees!) along the edge of the yard.

Dad planted little pine trees along the western side of the house that eventually grew into a huge windbreak of tall trees that helped protect the house from the fierce winter wind. Yes, the wind does whip across Iowa! In my lifetime on the farm, we were lucky to never have gotten the full force of a tornado, although we felt the tornado tail winds. I remember the time when the wind was so fierce that it blew the pouring rain into the house around one of the large upstairs bedroom windows, requiring all of us to scurry to sop up the rain pouring over the windowsill. We took turns sopping up water, ringing out rags and towels into buckets for what-seemed-like hours!

I was raised in a trusting time and place. Like our farm neighbors, our doors were never locked. I don't know if we even had a key to our farmhouse. I look back with much fondness to those days of innocence.

Dad (Art Schuessler) was the corn husking champion, locally and at the state level, for several years. His well- trained team of horses moved by his voice command. The corn had to be the most corn picked by hand and the cleanest corn.

Chapter 3
The Wider Circle

Sunup to sundown, there was always work to be done on the farm, except on Sundays. Sundays were a day of rest. Not even laundry was to be done. Only in very extreme circumstances did Dad ever work in the fields on a Sunday. We attended the Evangelical and Reformed Grace Church at Lone Tree every Sunday for two hours, first Sunday school and then the church service. We didn't just attend, as my parents were leaders in the congregation, singing in the choir, teaching Sunday School, and being officers in the congregation. I vividly remember how Mom threw herself into everything she did, even taking her high school Sunday School class for a week at Lake McBride every summer. I can't forget the church missionaries who came from all over the world and often stayed at our home, filling me with fascinating stories!

Grace Evangelical Reformed Church in Lone Tree, IA

31

Of course, we children followed in my parents' footsteps, deepening our church participation as we grew older. Hymn singing, and later, the choir formed the beginnings of my love of singing. Church is also where I widened my circle of friends. I think particularly of Mary Ann Lorack (Burr), my life-long friend, from childhood to today! One of my fondest Sunday memories was coming home from a long morning in church to one of Mom's tasty fried chicken dinners, which often included relatives or friends. I don't know how she managed to do all that, although I confess that I never gave it a thought at the time.

Most of my friends were from nearby farms whom I got to know well at our one room country school. There were usually twelve to fifteen students altogether in different grades, but all taught by one teacher. As a matter of course, the older students helped the younger ones. Our school was conveniently located on our farm, only about a quarter mile down the dirt road. We often just cut across the field and climbed the fence. Mom was the substitute teacher whenever we needed one. Dad was the director of the school and hired the teacher. The teacher lived with us during week days and went home every weekend. The Johnson County superintendent periodically would drop in to observe her, but we never knew when it would be.

*This is the country school that I went to that was on the family farm.
It was Lincoln #6-Grove School.*

My first teacher, Miss Murphy, was my favorite. I can picture her today! She was probably only about eighteen years old. On some weekends I went home with her to play with her little sister who happened to be about my age. At that time, women had to follow strict rules of behavior like never marrying and not smoking or drinking. Miss Murphy left our school after a few years when she got married. How I missed her!

Donna,5, Miss Murphy and Joanne, 7

I don't remember much about what I learned at country school, but I vividly recall recesses and music. We had an old victrola at school that we sang along with to learn such songs as "Jimmy (Jenny to me!) Crack Corn". Our one-room school was heated with a large pot-bellied stove in the middle of the room where we liked to sit to warm our feet. In order to use the outhouse, we had to go far out behind the school to the little shed with two holes and a catalogue in the days before toilet paper. As you can imagine, outhouses were "aromatic", so they were always some distance away.

The first cold, snowy day in kindergarten, I did not want to make the long walk to the outhouse, so I stayed at my desk and wet my pants. Marvin sat right behind me. The teacher made him clean up my mess, thinking he had left snow on his shoes that had melted. I sat by the stove to dry out my long, tan stockings, held up by a garter belt, that all girls wore in the cold winter. Each student brought a cold lunch in a metal lunch box. We also each brought a jar of water that was poured into a large ceramic container with a spigot, with a community tin cup for everyone to share. Some years later, Dad put in a pump near the schoolhouse so we would have water right there.

Sometimes, we'd hitch up our beloved pony, Patsy, to a cart and drive her to pick up the neighbor children for a ride to school in the morning. When we arrived at school, my brother, Marvin, tied the reins loosely to the cart, headed Patsy toward our home and patted her on the rear. She trotted up the road, up our long lane to Mom, who was waiting to unhitch her and put her in our pasture. Mom could see the school from our front yard, so she knew when to wait

34

for Patsy. I thought all ponies must be like Patsy, so gentle and well behaved.

Patsy taking us to school (Marvin is standing and I am sitting behind the wheel).

Even though there was a wide range of ages in country school, we all played together. As it happened, our school was at the base of a small hill on a dirt road that was not traveled much, so in winter we brought our wooden sleds to school and slid down that big hill. Marvin, Joanne, and I had two sleds, one small and the other big enough for two. We kids had great times making "trains" with our sleds, pulling the rope of the sled behind us while sliding down the hill. Sometimes, we invited other nearby country school children to join us in fun activities, even competing with them in softball games. I thought I must be pretty good since I always got to play third base!

We also played a game called Andy Over the School House, I think my favorite! One half of the students were on each side of the school house. One team threw a softball over the roof for the other team to try and catch. If they caught the ball, they ran around to the other side of the school to try and tag members of the opposing team. And if you were caught, you had to join their team until there was no one left on one side. We loved other games as well, like checkers, marbles, chalk board writing/drawing, dare base, and tag.

Some noon hours in the winter, the teacher allowed Marvin to check his animal traps in the creek, even letting Joanne and me to go with him. He caught mostly beavers, rabbits, and "coons". Later that evening, he collected them from the traps to bring home to dress, stretching the skins over a board to get them ready to sell. The worst part for me was that Joanne or I would have to hold them by their legs while he pulled the skin off! And the awful smell!

The school program was the highlight of our year. All students took part and all the parents would attend. Sometimes we each took a box lunch. The teacher would auction it off and then we would eat with whoever bought our box. I can still picture myself in my first program when I recited the poem, "I never saw a purple cow, I never hope to see one".

Those were wonderful carefree days, with my ever-expanding world of friends! How fortunate I was to grow up in a loving, safe place.

Phyllis Lenz, Donna, Mary Lenz, and Frances Lenz

Chapter 4
Fun Times

I loved doing things with my big brother, Marvin (four years older) and my big sister, Joanne (two years older). As the littlest one, I was always the tag-along, trying to keep up with them! I followed along with whatever they wanted to do. I learned to trust because they always looked out for me. As I look back, I think I spent much of my life trying to live up to them!

Jumping rope was a favorite thing for us. We learned different ways to jump rope with two ropes, or we would use one long rope with a person holding each end. We also played marble games, as well as board games like Monopoly and also card games. We loved playing outside with our big collie dog, Dixie. Dad built a tall rope swing with a board seat in one of the huge trees in the front yard. It made my stomach jump every time because it swung back and forth really high!

One summer day when I was about three years old, Marvin, Joanne, and I went to the cornfield to play Hide and Seek. Since it had rained the night before, the field was muddy, and Joanne and Marvin were running and sliding around the cornfield. They got pretty muddy, but I was still clean, so Joanne asked me if I wanted to get a "spanking" when we got back to the house?" I didn't understand what she was getting at, but it soon became clear that she wanted to change her muddy clothes into MY clean clothes. Now if Joanne asked me to do something, of course I agreed! We exchanged clothes, with me now wearing her muddy clothes, but no one got a spanking because I'm sure Mom figured out what had happened!

I longed for a play room, so when I was about eight years old, my mother agreed to let me transform a tiny upstairs storage room. We used all of the left-over strips of wallpaper from her previous papering jobs in the house. I loved it, but it makes me smile to think of what a patchwork of designs it was! I remember many happy hours playing in my new playroom with my dolls and the little table and chairs, as well as with my families of paper dolls that I cut from the Sears catalogue. I even found different outfits that fit them from the catalogue so I could change their clothes! You can imagine my excitement when the new catalogue arrived in the weeks before Christmas every year.

Christmas was a special time for us, but very different from today. It was not so much about gift exchanges, but more about presents from Santa Claus. On Christmas Eve, Mom helped Marvin, Joanne, and me to drape one of our long stockings (one of our actual stockings, not a special Christmas stocking) over a kitchen chair for Santa to fill with treats. The first thing we saw on Christmas morning was our filled stockings! In the bottom of each was an orange, then nuts in the shell, topped off with Christmas ribbon candies. I think the candies were mostly for looks because they were so pretty with their bright colors, but they were sickeningly sweet, even for me!

I loved the variety of nuts in the stocking, especially because of the fun of cracking them open. I thought nothing of it at the time, but we referred to the Brazil nuts as "nigger toes", not realizing that it was a mean and derogatory term. In fact, I'd never heard the word nigger so I didn't know what it meant. I'm guessing my parents did not know either, since by their actions and words, I never detected any racial prejudice from them.

And so it was that I was part of the institutional racism of American society and didn't even know it. I wonder in how many other ways?! I think of the rhyme we often recited, "Eeny, meeny, miny, moe, Catch a nigger by the toe". I see now how easily adults, often unwittingly, plant biases in children's minds. And to think that little girls like me, except with darker skin, would have heard such hurtful things!

We never expected more than one gift from Santa, usually a doll for us little girls, but one year, Joanne and I each got a pretty buggy with a doll inside! When we were a little older, we each got a gold heart-shaped locket that opened. So special to me, but to my horror, I dropped it through the heat register in the living room! Dad came to my rescue, unscrewing the register to retrieve it! Then there was the Christmas that my parents sent us outside on Christmas morning to find a brown and white pony for all three of us! That was our dear Patsy!

Joanne and I got a doll AND buggy for that Christmas!

39

Halloween was also a fun time for us, but costumes were not part of our Halloween tradition when we snuck up to neighbors' houses. Marvin, Joanne, and I would walk the deserted country roads carrying bagsful of shelled field corn from our farm. We were as quiet as mice outside the house, so the family would not know we were there. Then we'd toss a handful of the hard kernels against a window of the neighbor's house to get their attention, and quickly run and hide behind the bushes or whatever. The family knew they had to come find us! If we were lucky, they'd give us a little treat when they found us.

Dressing up for Halloween-Donna, Joanne,
neighbor-Geraldine Wissink, and Marvin

Although it was a rather insular life on the farm, my parents regularly connected with family. Aunts, uncles, and cousins were an important part of our lives as we began to travel greater distances to visit them. They would visit us as well, often arriving at our door unannounced! Even if they showed up at a mealtime, they knew they were always welcome to join us. It could be a lonely life, so I think farm families were happy to have company. I can still hear Mom say, "My nose is itching so we must be going to have company".

I do not remember ever having a baby sitter since we always tagged along with our parents. I remember how farmers and their wives loved to dance (my parents being no exception!) and would find their way on Saturday nights to the Circle Inn, the home of an old-fashioned barn dance on a farm about three miles away. The barn had been made over into a beautiful, huge dance floor on the top floor with a little combo or a lady playing all the familiar tunes on the piano. We walked down the tall outside steps of the barn to the bottom floor where they sold refreshments.

What a wonderful time everyone had dancing! The Bunny Hop and the Hokey Pokey were especially fun for us kids. There was a long wooden bench built along the walls of the dance floor, so as the evening wore on and we got tired, we just laid down on the bench and fell asleep. The Circle Inn must have been known far and wide as it is documented that even Lawrence Welk and Guy Lombardo played with their bands there, braving the often-muddy roads.

Mom and Dad also enjoyed regular card playing nights with four or five neighbor families, usually preceded by a yummy potluck dinner. Each card table was assigned a number and set up around the host home. After each round of cards, everyone changed partners, while the winning partners at each table would move up to the next table. Each person had a scorecard that they took with them as they rotated through the tables. They even had little prizes at the end of the evening, first place, second place, and "booby prize".

Of course, all of the children came too, sometimes playing hide-and-seek outside and catching lightening bugs for bright rings or bracelets. When we got to be eight or ten years old, we were invited to play cards with adults. They were very understanding and helpful to us as we were just learning to play cards. I'm proud to say, I got quite good at Bid Euchre, and acquired a love of playing cards throughout my life!

Most Wednesday evenings in the summer, Mom and Dad would take us to Lone Tree where they would join other locals to hear the town band play in the park. We children would head over to the cinema house to see a movie, afterwards just hanging out around town, often at Marner's drug store. When I was very little, I had heard people order ice cream there, telling the drug store clerk to "charge it." Although my parents never ran a tab for store charges, I decided to try asking the clerk for an ice cream cone that way, telling him to "just charge it". He always gave it to me. After a while, my parents began to figure out how I got the ice cream cone. Eventually Dad went to the drug store and paid my ice cream bill. The clerk and he had a good laugh, but I learned never to do that again!

Farm families also had a mischievous sense of fun, surprising newly married couples into the neighborhood by serenading them with a "chivaree", a loud banging of pots, pans, or other noisemakers. It was prearranged that we would all very quietly gather in their front yard one evening and then start making a ruckus! The noise eventually brought the young couple outside to meet their new neighbors, often bringing snacks out for everyone.

Dad suffered with hay fever every summer, and in the absence of antihistamines, he would sometimes have to sleep in the cool cellar in a chair at night in order to breathe. But the hay fever seemed to disappear as soon as we crossed out of Iowa! And so it was that after the summer/fall crops were all in, we piled in the car and headed west.

We went to the Black Hills, the Badlands, and other places as far as Denver. There were no hotels, only very rustic cabin-type motels. Mom always took her electric skillet and some food. We usually had a cold meat sandwich at a park along the road for lunch. Mom cooked something to eat in our skillet for supper. Sometimes we even got to eat in a restaurant for supper which was a big deal!

One of the scariest times in my life was when I was about ten years old. We had just left Denver and were going over Granite Pass in the Rocky Mountains, heading for California. The roads over the mountains were all gravel at that time with hairpin curves. Dad was making one of those sharp turns on the outside of the mountain going up when our old 40s era black Dodge slid partway off the road because of the loose gravel.

We were very close to the edge, so Dad told all of us to get out of the car VERY slowly so we wouldn't tip the car off the side of the mountain! After we all got out, I seem to remember Marvin even pushed the car to help Dad to get it back on the road. I'll never forget Dad's announcement to us that evening when we got to a motel, that we were no longer going to California. Instead, we were heading back down the mountain a different way and going straight home!

And so, despite some scary moments, I have wonderful childhood memories with my parents and siblings. I didn't mind being the littlest one, always trying to keep up with

Joanne and Marvin, though the time would come when I needed to become my own person.

Donna and Joyce, 4, at Colorado Springs

Joanne, Mom, Dad and Joyce in Colorado

PART 2

Coming of Age
1945-1955

"I am only one, but still I am one. I cannot do everything, but still I can do something. And because I cannot do everything, I will not refuse to do something that I can do."
Edward Everett Hale

Donna-Eighth Grade-1948

Chapter 5
The Times

America was booming after the ending of WWII in 1945. No more ration books, but nevertheless, my "waste not, want not" mentality stayed with me for life. A different kind of global tension was on the horizon, the Cold War between the U.S and the Soviet Union, and along with it, the anti-Communist hysteria began spreading across our country. All of this, I was only peripherally aware of then since I was focused on finding my way in approaching my adulthood!

Segregation was prevalent throughout the country then, especially in the South, but since we did not have any black families in our community, I was largely unaware of the harsh realities. When televisions began to creep into homes, we learned of changes that were afoot when Jackie Robinson made history in 1947, becoming the first African American in baseball's major leagues. And to think that in my lifetime, we went from segregation to having a black President, a black vice-president and a black woman on the Supreme Court!

Keep in mind that the roles of men and women were quite clearly defined back then, husbands being the head of the family as the breadwinner, while wives supported their husbands, tending to the cooking, cleaning, and the children. That path was laid out for me as a teenager, so I was determined to prepare myself to become the best wife and mother I could be!

At age ten, I followed in Joanne's footsteps, joining our neighborhood 4-H club, the Fremont Lassies. It was a wonderful preparation for us girls, learning "wifely" skills like sewing, cooking, and woodworking. The club was organized around the planning and making of various projects. We learned so much then that carried me through the rest of my life!

Every summer, area 4-H clubs gathered for a week at the Johnson County 4-H Fair, giving demonstrations of our projects. Judges rated each demonstration with a ribbon (blue, red, or white) and determined which were worthy to be presented at the Iowa State Fair in Des Moines. I was usually very shy, but these 4-H demonstrations helped me feel at ease in speaking in front of a group. Joanne and I were lucky enough to take at least one project to the state fair every year, and such an honor it was. We even became Johnson County 4-H officers in our high school years.

Donna(12) with her 4H projects

Single women were rare in our little community, but one of Dad's sisters never married. Remember the card game "Old Maid"? The term "old maid" was used at that time to refer to women like my Aunt Laura. Her face had been scarred by scalding water in a home accident when she was just a girl, so she may have felt she wasn't pretty enough to attract a husband. In any case, I always thought she was lovely, and Joanne and I took turns staying with her whenever we had after-school activities in high school.

I remember that Aunt Laura was so much fun, often giggling with her to the point that I couldn't stop! But I know it must have been a difficult life for her with no husband to support her, as was the custom of the day. There were few job opportunities for women then, but I know she worked for a time as a waitress at the Lone Tree café. Later, she became the caretaker of Grandpa Schuessler in his declining years. I remember Mom and Dad helped her out with food and essentials whenever they could.

Aunt Laura Schuessler-1965

Even though Joanne and I knew that marriage and children were in our future, Mom made it clear to us that we needed to have a way to support ourselves and our children should anything happen to our husbands. Her thinking was years ahead of the Women's Liberation Movement of the '60s, but I have no doubt that she had been affected by seeing one of her sisters struggle when her husband died. That is how it came to be that after high school, I went to Iowa State Teachers College to become a teacher, something that sustained me throughout my life.

It wasn't until I was in high school that we got our first TV set. It was an exciting time as we were one of the first in our area to get one! It opened up our world, although it had only three channels, one of which was often too "snowy" to watch! Another problem was a seemingly constant need to adjust the screen with a button on back of the TV to keep the picture from "scrolling".

TVs back then were free-standing consoles with a small screen, maybe fifteen inches square. Ours had "rabbit ears" on top that we used to move around to try to make the picture come in better.   Even though they were so often difficult to see clearly, we loved watching our favorite shows, like Ed Sullivan, Milton Berle, Dinah Shore, the Lone Ranger, and Gene Autry. Mom loved the Kate Smith Show ("When the Moon Comes Over the Mountain" and "God Bless America"), Dad developed a routine of watching professional baseball every Sunday afternoon, and of course we never missed the nightly news.

Naturally, I was becoming increasingly aware of boys and the prospects of dating. At that time, the word SEX was never spoken of by our parents or even in our community, so I had to pretty much figure things out on my own. There was no such thing as sex education in our school, but thankfully I had my older sister, Joanne, as my confidant. Nevertheless, it was all very mysterious and yet wonderful!

Romance and sex did not equate in my mind when I was in high school. The closest thing we got to touching was dancing, and dance we did, almost every Saturday night! This time in my life was the era of the Big Bands, like Benny Goodman and Glenn Miller. Rock and Roll was quickly taking over the teen scene, although I still preferred the dance music of the Big Bands. I didn't know what to make of Elvis's gyrations at the time!

Reflective of the attitudes about women and sexuality, it was not considered appropriate, or even allowed at school, for girls to wear slacks. We only wore long dresses or skirts, certainly nothing that revealed our female shape. Of course, spandex had yet to be invented, but such things would have been too provocative for us to wear! And even though I weighed only a hundred-twenty pounds at the time, we girls

 always wore a girdle. How times have changed!

Joanne, Joyce (1 year), Marvin and Donna-1948

Chapter 6
My Broadening World

My world seemed to burst open when I began attending sixth grade at the community school in Lone Tree. My parents had decided it was time for us kids to leave country school for a better education and more socialization. It was difficult to leave such wonderful times at country school, but I was ready for new friends and adventures.

There were no school buses at first, so my parents paid Fritz Kruger, a friend of Marvin's and a neighbor who lived about a mile away, to let us ride with him the four and a half miles to town school. It seems odd to me now, but I remember we had to walk a mile to and from his house each morning and afternoon to get a ride with him.

Driving the ten minutes into Lone Tree was considered a major trip at the time. I don't remember any local family having more than one car, so driving back and forth was kept to a minimum. My parents made it clear that you did not "run into town" every time you wanted something, but waited until there were several errands you could accomplish in one trip. That kind of thinking would serve us well today with skyrocketing gas prices and worries about climate change!

Lone Tree (population 650) was like Walnut Grove for Laura Ingalls Wilder, the hub of social and commercial activity for the surrounding area. The town was named after the huge elm tree that stood alone on the prairie there as a landmark for pioneers going west. And although it succumbed to Dutch elm disease in later years, you can find pictures of the majestic tree at the Lone Tree Historical Society today. Where the tree once stood is now just a stump with a gold plaque.

THE Lone Tree

Lone Tree was laid out with businesses along both sides of the main street (Devoe Street), while houses lined the side streets. Just before entering Lone Tree from the north on Highway 218, you see the town cemetery on the left and the Lone Tree Park on the right. Next, you cross the railroad tracks that used to carry farmers' grain to market, though the tracks have long since been removed.

Immediately to the right was a lumberyard and just past it, a smaller park with a bandstand, a favorite gathering place. Nearby was the grain elevator where the farmers brought their grain to market, and across the street was the only bank in town, where farmers went for their loans to purchase seeds for their next crop. Further up the street on the right was Ross's Dry Goods, a small crowded store with an assortment of household items like sheets and towels, a few clothes (mostly underwear) with a space at the back for trying on shoes. I don't remember ever entering that store when Mr. and Mrs. Ross were not there to assist us. It was truly a mom-and-pop business!

At the corner was Marner's drugstore, which sold first aid supplies, a few over-the-counter medicines like aspirin and cough drops, greeting cards, and a variety of candy. It also had a soda fountain where you could get an ice cream cone and a cherry coke, which made it a popular spot for us young folks! Around the corner from the drugstore was Young's Insurance Agency and the office of the Lone Tree Reporter, our weekly newspaper. Sorden and Adams Furniture store. across the street, doubled as a funeral home.

Krall's grocery store (not resembling a supermarket!) was owned by Janet Krall's parents, a classmate of mine. Most days, you could see older men in town sitting on the wooden bench in front of the store, chewing tobacco. Sometimes I noticed a little boy sitting with them. I found out much later, after I got married, that the little boy was my future husband, Don Bean, whose grandpa lived in town. His grandpa bought raisins for him to chew, so he could chew "tobacco" like the men. His grandpa had even been mayor of Lone Tree for some years.

The Lone Tree Cinema was a favorite place for us teenagers. Nearby was Rife's barbershop, owned and operated by Mary Lou Rife's dad, also a classmate of mine. Further along the street was Schnoebelen's gas station, and across from that was the Lone Tree café and the two taverns. These taverns were mysterious places to me, and although I only went past the door to peek inside, they seemed to be dimly lit and smoke-filled. It was an unwritten understanding that women and children were not to go inside! I believe they served beer and sandwiches, but it was also a gathering place for playing cards, which Dad liked to do, much to my mother's consternation!

Dr. Mossman was the town veterinarian and Dr. Jacques, the town doctor, whose offices were housed in their homes. Dr. Jacques continued to make house calls then, but office visits were slowly becoming the norm.

At the edge of town sat the Lone Tree Community School (kindergarten through twelfth grade), a huge red brick building with an adjoining gymnasium, a playground, and a baseball diamond. The school was immensely important in local lives, serving not only as a place where the surrounding community came together for school happenings, but also as a spot for community events like community baseball games. I was proud that my dad was the pitcher for the town team then, which competed against other nearby towns.

Lone Tree School and Gym in 1952. It burned down on Christmas day, 1956 and a new school was rebuilt. The gym is the only part that survived the fire.

There were also three churches in town, nestled among the houses, the Evangelical and Reformed church where we attended, the Methodist church, and Saint Mary's Catholic church. I knew that dating (or marrying!) a Catholic boy would not be acceptable to Mom. She told me that if I were to have a mixed religion marriage, my children would have to be raised in the Catholic faith, not mine. That was the closest thing to prejudice I had heard from my parents.

Lone Tree was such a warm and friendly place to grow up. My parents taught us by their example that "it does not hurt" to say hello or to wave at anyone, even if we don't know them! You can imagine how easy it was for me to make new friends, many I've kept for a lifetime! Later, my husband, Don, recalled that when he came to see me at our house, he always waved to everyone he saw along the way, since he knew they were either a friend or a relative of mine!

During my teenage years, I thought nothing about walking the four-and-a-half miles to/from Lone Tree, but on more than a few occasions, I was given a ride from someone driving my direction. In fact, hitchhiking was fairly common for us kids because we knew most everyone, but of course, we never accepted a ride from a stranger! Marvin had his own bike which he rode to town sometimes, but Joanne and I shared a bike.

A life-changing event took place when I was thirteen years old, when Mom and Dad told me I would be having a sibling! I would no longer be "the baby of the family"! It was one of the greatest days of my life when, on April 20, 1947, my baby sister, Joyce, was born! A wonderfully exciting time in my life!

At that time, women stayed in the hospital for about a week when they had a baby, so while Mom was away, we planned a surprise for her return home. Marvin, Joanne, and I took on the daunting task of planting our huge garden ourselves (with Dad's supervision of course!). It took days to complete, but Mom was so pleased to see what we had done!

I doted on my new baby sister, spending lots of time holding, rocking, and feeding her. Not to say that Joyce couldn't be a pain at times when she got a little older, like the time she hid my gold strappy high-heeled shoes right before I had to leave for a formal date! None-the-less, I always felt I was her second mother, a feeling that has lasted to this day! I am so grateful to have had this very special bond with her throughout our lives.

A couple years after Joyce's birth, our family suddenly grew again when two of my cousins, Mary, age six, and Betty, age four, came to live with us. Only much later in my life did I become more aware of the trauma that had befallen their young lives, but at the time, I only knew that their father had died of throat cancer and that their mother, Mom's sister, Elva, had an emotional breakdown as a result. I can only imagine the struggle it must have been for Aunt Elva to be thrust with the care and support of her four young children on her own, when she had been accustomed to a secure married life with a full-time nanny.

And so it was that her four small children were split among Mom and her siblings, David going to live with Uncle Myron and Aunt Dora, Fred with Aunt Edna and Uncle Jim, and Mary and Betty coming to live with us. I know that the upheaval and distress they experienced had to have taken a toll, but that makes my admiration for them even greater. They were, and still are, very special to me, growing into such caring and loving women!

Mary Malone, Joyce and Betty Malone-1950

You can see that I was drawn to babies and children, so it followed that I was in demand as a babysitter in my high school days. Some summers, I took care of my three young Heither cousins, often staying at their house for a week at a time. I was a regular sitter for our close neighbors, Doris and Harold Schuessler, as well as Arlyne and Duane Stock. I lived with Stocks for a month after Arlyne came home from the hospital with their third child, Gary. I only went home on weekends that month, even catching the school bus from their house.

Duanie, Gary and Susie Stock at the piano. At times, I lived with them as a nanny and even caught the school bus at their house, through high school. They were like my second family.

I also babysat quite often for our minister's son, Phillip. I felt lucky to be there to take care of Phillip when he accompanied his mother all around the area with her amazing talking bird shows! It was quite a hit everywhere she took her show with so many different kinds of parrots, and I was there to see it all!

The Sunday school that I taught in 1952. I'm not in the picture because I was taking it. No selfies back then!

My involvement in church continued to deepen. I sang in the church choir, was active in our Youth Fellowship, taught Sunday School each week and Bible School for two weeks every summer, and even subbed as organist for services. Joanne and I, along with my dear friend, Mary Ann Lorack

(Burr), were actively involved in church camp for two weeks every summer. The importance of a caring church family stayed with me for the rest of my life.

Graduation from church camp in 1952.

New friend Wilma and Mary Anne Lorack with me on the right.

During these years, my family began to branch out to the "big city" of Iowa City, about fifteen miles from our farm, with a population approaching 20,000.   It was a major outing when we went to Iowa City, only traveling there once in a while for shopping at its big stores. We went for the day, and got to have lunch at the counter at Woolworth's Dime Store where Dad invariably ordered his favorite hot beef sandwich with mashed potatoes. Before we left to go home, we often stopped at the Old Mill Ice Cream shop where I got a huge five-cent ice cream cone. My special treat!

When we arrived at Iowa City, we often split up to go our separate ways, agreeing upon a time to meet later at the Jefferson Hotel. The hotel was a favorite meeting place for many people, as it was located on a corner near all the downtown stores, with a huge lounging area laid out in groupings of couches and overstuffed chairs. I remember being fascinated to watch as people got into the Jefferson's elevator, though I never got to ride in it.

Iowa City had a bit of a cosmopolitan flavor to it, as it was the home of the University of Iowa with students from all over the world. In fact, the University's student body almost equaled the population of the city. You can imagine how interesting a place it was to a young girl from the farm. Imagine a country girl growing up with a little window into the wider world!

Joanne, Marvin and Donna
Ready to take on the world!

Chapter 7
High School

I seemed to "find myself" during high school. I had spent my childhood as the little sister of Joanne, whom I looked up to and did my best to emulate. Being just two years younger, I was involved in so many things with her, like church, 4-H, and piano lessons. It was natural that I would want to live up to her standards, but that was a tall order because she was a stand-out, especially in basketball and her piano playing.

Mrs. Nelson, my high school music teacher, was one of those people who changed everything for me. She took a particular interest and opened up a new world for me. She knew that I loved to sing, and surprised me one day by telling me that I had a good singing voice! At her suggestion, my parents let me switch from piano to voice lessons with her. I had found something that set me apart, a gift that gave me a way to shine away from the shadow of anyone else!

Sue Petsel and I often sang together. She played the marimba and piano well. Sometime I would be asked to sing on the roof of the Iowa City Drive-in Theater and she would play the piano for me.

I was chosen to sing many solos, compete in yearly state contests, and to join our school trio and sextet as well as both girls' chorus and mixed chorus. My newfound ability spilled over outside school, singing at many local weddings and funerals. I also sang numerous times at the nearby Iowa City drive-in theater. They invited people to entertain between movies many weekends, and somehow, they got my name. My friend, Sue Petzel, often accompanied me on the piano on those occasions, singing such favorites as "Side by Side". I was always nervous, but I enjoyed it so much! Not surprisingly, singing became part of me, carrying me throughout my life!

Another high school teacher, Mrs. Dalton, recognized that I had done well in my business classes all four years of high school, like bookkeeping, short-hand, and typing. I was, in fact, one of the fastest typists at school! My senior year, Mrs. Dalton asked if I would like to take off a few hours each week from school to volunteer at a local business, and I was delighted! It was great "on the job training" which allowed me to get secretarial jobs down the road, during college and summers between teaching. My typing skills also came in very handy throughout my teaching career!

I know I was fortunate to be at a small school that afforded so many opportunities to me. Besides music, I was very involved on the school paper staff, which had a school news column each week in the Lone Tree Reporter. I also had fun on our school basketball team all four years. I have to admit that our basketball team was not the greatest, but our coach, Mr. Whylie, instilled in us the notion that the importance of playing was to have fun, not just to win! Little did I know then that I would have the same fun in my elder years on a Granny Basketball team!

My HS basketball team Back row-Donna third from left,
Joanne second from right

Girls' basketball was much different when I was in high school, with each team member playing on only half the court, three forwards on one side and three guards on the other. I always played front guard, since I was short. Lone Tree had one of the best gymnasiums of all the schools in area towns, so we always hosted the district competitions. At the time, girls' basketball was not usually offered at the large high schools in Iowa.

Throughout these years, Mom and Dad encouraged us kids in all our activities, attending every event that Marvin, Joanne and I participated in. They sat through long piano recitals, all school music events, and our basketball games. It meant so much to me to see them in the audience!

At our girls' basketball games, Shirley Watkinson (King), one of my dearest friends to this day, always sold popcorn and snacks for the school, to folks watching in the bleachers. When my girl's game was over, I joined her selling popcorn during the boys' basketball game. I also remember how much fun she and I had doing gymnastics during the noon recess in the school yard. We spent many hours at each other's home. She had a creek on her farm where we went ice skating every winter. It's funny to think back how our ice skates clamped onto our shoes back then, as did our roller skates.

Other school friends pop into my head like Sondra Kline (Schnoebelen), Janet Krall (Vincent), Wayne Jarrard, Betty Becker (Forbes), Audrey Brenneman (Dodson), Shirley Watkinson (King), and Mary Ann Lorack (Burr), who was my first best friend from my younger days at Sunday School. I always remember how Dale Johnson got me through geometry and algebra!

At that time, sons of farmers generally followed their fathers into farming, so some family names were becoming prominent in the area, like Hotz, Lenz, Burr, and Schuessler. I never thought about it at the time, but I think that being a "Schuessler girl" gave me confidence and helped me fit in with everyone.

My high school class of thirty-one students was the largest to graduate from Lone Tree at that point. I think we were an unusually cohesive group, doing so many things together and planning future events. We all seemed to have similar attitudes and behavior, not experimenting with alcohol or cigarettes as some classes did. I don't remember anyone being excluded or bullied. The ones living in this area still meet once a month for lunch yet today.

Can you find me? I am in the 2nd row from the bottom, 3rd from left.

At one of our class meetings as freshmen, we made a goal to earn enough money by our senior year to take a class trip to Detroit, Michigan and go through the car factory. At that time, our families did not have the money to support such frivolity, so throughout the years leading up to our senior trip, our class seemed to be constantly having money-making events like bake/donut sales. Not surprisingly, we were successful in reaching our goal with thirty cents left over!

It's funny how certain experiences from my youth stick in my head. I remember one day when a teacher looked my way with an angry expression on her face, stomping down the aisle, toward me. I wondered what I had done, but was relieved when she grabbed the boy behind me and shook him! A scary moment!

One day, I got in trouble when a group of us classmates saw test questions on a teacher's desk and someone reported it to the teacher. She gave each of us a note home to return with our parent's signature. I was dreading to go home, but my parents were matter of fact about it. They discussed it with me and signed the note. I never wanted to do anything that made me feel that dishonest again!

When I was a sophomore, a small group of high school kids was starting up a new band to play at dance halls in the area and asked me if I'd like to play piano with them. Of course, I was honored. With my parents' approval, I decided to try it! We were named, "The Prairie Landers." The only problem was, I needed music and the others all played by ear. After playing for a few months, I told the group that I would rather be out there dancing! There were no hard feelings from anyone. I had tried something that just wasn't a good fit for me.

I got my driver's license during high school, but there was no such thing as Driver's Education, of course. I don't remember actually learning to drive, as I had been used to driving a tractor on the farm for so many years. There were many dirt roads around Lone Tree at the time, three within a mile of our farm. These un-graveled roads could be a challenge for an inexperienced driver, as it proved to be for me one morning when I was driving Mom and my sister, Joyce, to a 4-H gathering.

It had rained a little the night before, but the road seemed fine at first. But when we got a little further along, the car began to slide from side to side, while I tried everything to keep it on the road! Finally, I could only think to put on the brake to stop the car, but that was the last thing I should have done, as Mom told me afterwards.

We ended up in the deep ditch, the car at a steep angle. The three of us just sat and looked at each other, wondering how we were going to get out of this predicament. To this day, I don't remember what we did, but it was probably a kind farmer with his tractor and a chain that pulled us out. I remember Dad having to go out many a night to do that same thing for someone who knocked on our door, asking for help to get his car out of the ditch!

Family reunions were an important part of my life all through my life. Every summer, Mom planned two family reunions, one for her relatives, the Boyles, and one for dad's relatives, the Schuesslers. Folks came from near and far, so many that we had to use the church basement or nearby park, to hold such a gathering! To start things off, we always had a wonderful dinner, with everyone bringing something to share.

The Boyle Siblings-
Myron, Edith, Ransom
(Ranny), Elva Malone
and Edna Weir

The adults chatted and laughed together while the kids played games. We always had some music to finish off the day, often joining in together on favorite hymns. The Schuesslers, in particular, loved their old German songs, so either Joanne or I always played the piano to accompany. It was such fun for us to get together with family, especially those that we rarely got to see!

I always had a strong connection to children, and when I was old enough, I was a sought-after babysitter. On one occasion when I was a senior in high school, one of our neighbors, Arlyne and Duane Stock, had arranged for me to watch their little ones while they went to a local dance. However, they changed their minds when I told them that my boyfriend's band was playing there that night. They got someone else to take my place, babysitting the children and invited me to go with them to the dance and surprise him!

It was indeed a surprise! When we arrived at the dance, several of my friends rushed up to me to say that my "steady" boyfriend (LaVon) had come with another girl that night! I was so hurt to learn that he had deceived me! At the time, we were wearing each other's class rings and planning our future together. I simply took off his ring and set it on the bandstand without saying a word. This is the first time in my life I lost trust in another person, so you can imagine my heartbreak, though it was an important life lesson for me!

Of course, I was disappointed not to have a date for my upcoming senior prom. Mom suggested I call my cousin, Jimmy Weir, who lived near Muscatine, to see if he would like to take me to the prom. He was the same age as me, and we had always been good friends. None of my school friends had ever met him, and he was quite good looking, I recall! I do not think (unless they read this book) that anyone at the dance knew he was my cousin! LaVon's band was playing for our dance that night, so I really wanted him to think that I had met someone new!

I had grown tremendously as a person in high school, with a world of singing open to me. I felt ready to leave "the nest" and head to college for a career in teaching, eager to gain new friends and experiences. I'll be forever grateful to Mom for urging Joanne and me to prepare for our future, whether it be with or without a man in our lives.

My High School Graduation-1952

Chapter 8
Leaving Home

Just two weeks after my high school graduation in 1952, I was off and running! I left home to begin my studies at Iowa State Teachers' College, today's University of Northern Iowa. I was full of anticipation, and yet, a little nervous about making such a big change! It helped that the college was only about an hour-and-a half drive from my home, so I was able to be with family many weekends. It didn't feel quite so scary that way, and it also helped that I had arranged for a high school classmate, Betty Skala (Metz) to be my dormitory roommate.

At that time, students could be certified to teach after just two years of college. I planned it out so that I would graduate early, attending college straight through summers to get my degree. But no amount of planning could have accounted for the fact that a health condition almost prevented me from graduating. About one week before the final exams of my very first quarter, I noticed that the base of my tailbone was painful and getting a little worse every day.

The doctor at the college advised me to see my regular doctor at home, but without a car, finding rides was part of a student's routine then. Now, I could always find a ride to Iowa City, so my parents picked me up there and took me straight to Dr. Jacques. He told me that I had a pilonidal cyst on my tailbone that was abscessed. I could feel how swollen it had become, puffed up at the base of my tailbone!

I was devastated to learn that I had to have surgery to remove the cyst as soon as possible, but I still needed to take my final exams for that quarter! I could tolerate the pain at that time, so Mom and Dad took me back to college to take the tests. But within days, the pain got much worse, and I knew there was no way I could stay in school. I was determined not to lose my class credit for that quarter, so despite the pain, I went to see my school advisor, Miss Sparrow, to see what I could arrange.

Miss Sparrow told me that I had to get written permission from the teacher of each of my four courses in order to delay my final exams until after my surgery. I remember it was a steamy hot day when I trudged across the campus from one teacher to the next, with tears in my eyes from the now excruciating pain. Miss Sparrow felt so bad when I returned to her with the permission papers, not realizing that I was so sick!

After the surgery and a week at Mercy Hospital in Iowa City, I went home to recover for about three weeks. I confess that there were times when I was ready to give up. The surgery left a big open cut that hurt every time I sat, so I had to sit sideways to make it bearable. I had to follow a routine of twice daily soaks in the tub, afterwards repacking the wound with gauze. Mom helped me at first and eventually I could pack it myself.

I was determined to return to college in the fall to take my final exams from the previous quarter. Looking back, I don't know how I was able to continue the twice-daily soaking in the tub through all of this. Lots of times, I couldn't find time to eat lunch! On one of my periodic follow-up visits to Dr. Jacques, he told me that it was not healing properly (from the inside out), so I ended up having two more of the same surgeries before it finally healed correctly! We didn't have medical insurance back then, so Dr. Jacques very kindly did not charge my parents for the last surgery. After the third and final surgery, I took off an entire quarter of college to give myself time to heal properly. That seemed to make the difference, but even today, almost seventy years later, I am careful to ensure that that area does not get sore or irritated.

In spite of the surgeries, I made many good friends in college, singing for several of their weddings. Dorm life agreed with me, even with several roommate changes. My last roommate, Evelyn Smith, had a lasting impact on my life. I had known her brother, Don, who had asked me if I would consider rooming with his sister, as she was rather shy. That was one of best things I ever did, even getting an apartment with her when we got our first teaching jobs. My friend, Evelyn, will always have a special place in my heart!

Evelyn and Donna in college

In my last year, I was chosen to be an advisor for the freshman girls' dorm, to help them in any way I could. I remember one girl was very homesick and didn't want to be away in college. Through many long talks, I told her that college seemed important to her, and to my delight, she stayed! I found out years later, she eventually became a professor at the college!

I started out taking classes to become a music teacher, but that changed after I found out that a music teacher was expected to put together school music programs all the time! I switched to an elementary classroom teaching major, but I did continue with voice lessons and singing in both the acapella choir and the large college choir, as well as the chapel choir.

At the time, elementary classroom teachers had to demonstrate a little piano and singing background with a simple song. Easy for me, but not so for one of my friends who asked me to help her to pass the music test. Since I had grown up with music, I was surprised that she had only a three-note singing range and couldn't play the piano at all. Her determination made up for her lack of skills, paying close attention to everything I taught her. It was rewarding for me to work with her several times a week in the practice room I had reserved. I think it meant as much to me as it did to her when she passed the test!

During my second year in college, a friend sent in my name to sing on the Ted Mack Amateur Hour, a local TV show in Davenport. An exciting prospect for me! Mom and Dad picked me up at college for the audition. It was a nerve-wracking experience, but there was nothing to lose except our time and the gas to go. I did not, however, make the cut to appear on the show. Another learning experience!

Because of my surgeries, I was able to fulfill my physical education requirement only through class observations and successful completion of the tests, but I was unable to take electives in physical education, as I had hoped. I had planned that college was going to be a time when I would be able to learn the sports I had never had, like tennis and golf, but it was not to be.

Who would have known that this disappointment would turn out to be a blessing to me ten years later when I returned to college to get a four-year degree at the University of Iowa?! Instead of the PE classes I had intended to take at college, I took my electives in psychology and sociology, a newfound interest of mine. The University of Iowa accepted these credits all those years later, enough for a minor degree! These classes also provided me a strong background in working successfully with staff, parents, and students in my teaching career. You just never know!

My business skills from high school landed me a student job as a secretary for the Head of Education at college, Dr. Bishop. He and his full-time secretary were so kind to me, assigning me the task of organizing his office library to match the college library, as well as doing regular secretarial work like shorthand dictation and typing. While I was student teaching in Waterloo, I worked serving evening meals in the school cafeteria, since my office job hours did not fit with my student teaching hours.

While in college, I struck up a friendship with a boy who was in several of my classes who lived at home near the college. We both enjoyed dancing and going to movies, and he often asked if I could find a girl for a friend of his so we could double date. The obvious choice was my roommate, Evelyn, promising her that if she agreed, I would do the same for her someday. Years later that day came, after we got our first jobs together, when Evelyn asked me to go on a double date with a friend of a guy she was interested in.   That blind date turned out to be my future husband, Don Bean!

Don came to visit me in college-1954

It was during this time that I got a call from an old friend, Bob Carter, asking me out. I had first noticed him years earlier when I was still in high school. Mom used to drop Joanne and me off at a roller-skating rink in West Liberty while she visited many of her older relatives.   I was too shy to talk to Bob at the skating rink, but I loved to watch him, even skating backwards!

75

Somehow, he got my name, and later on, came to a couple of my high school basketball games. At one point he asked to take me home, but of course, at the time I was going steady with LaVon. So it was a surprise to hear from Bob again when I was at college, asking if I was free to date him now. He was an even better dancer than he was a roller-skater, so smooth with all the dances (waltz, fox trot, polka, and even the rumba!). So much fun! We became great dance partners and eventually began to talk about a future together.

However, things were complicated by the fact that Bob had joined the Navy, and came home only twice a year. We made an agreement that during the weeks while he was home on leave, we would date exclusively, but while he was away, we could see other people. Even when he was home, our dorms had a 10 PM curfew, but if any of us got back late from a date, the girls on the first floor always let us in through a window!

Sometimes I was able to get a room for Bob in the boys' dorm when he was back on leave. Travel was not so simple then, when most families had only one car, and we students didn't have a car of our own. We depended on the college bulletin board to see who might be going our way. It seemed I could usually find a ride to Iowa City, not so far from our farm, since it was a popular destination, and my parents would pick me up there. So different from today when students usually have their own car and take off whenever and wherever!

Long distance relationships were more difficult then too, in a world without cell phones, texting, or even private phones in dorm rooms. We had just one phone for the entire floor, and a pay phone at that! Oftentimes when Bob called, an operator would come on the line and say, "Your time is up. You will be disconnected unless you deposit the change for five more minutes". Whenever the hall phone rang, any of the girls who happened to be nearby would answer it, either yelling down the long hallway or getting the person from her room. Picture me just sitting on the hard floor in the hallway talking to my boyfriend!

In any case, before Bob got out of the Navy, I had started dating my future husband, Don, who like me, grew up on a farm and had a career in teaching. Don was a few years older than me, reminding me a bit of my dad, and offered the stability I needed in my life. I felt so badly when I eventually had to make a phone call to Bob, ending our relationship. It was one of the most difficult things I have had to do in my life!

I took an unexpected detour on my way from college to teaching. It was apparent that I would not be graduating until January because of time off for my surgeries. Not such a big deal, except that teaching jobs were more plentiful in the fall when the school year begins. I really wanted to get started with my teaching career right away, so that summer while I was recovering from my third surgery, I applied and got a job in nearby Kalona, with the promise that I would return to college for my teaching degree the following summer.

As it happened, the chair of the Kalona Board of Education, Mr. Skola, asked if I would be willing to take a secretarial job at the Kalona Bank, where he was the president, for the summer before I started teaching. It seemed doable to me as the job did not appear to be physically strenuous since I was still recovering. My secretarial skills from high school came in handy once again! I loved it! I found a room in Mrs. Tilden's upstairs, eating every meal out. Mr. and Mrs. Skola invited me to go out with them and their two young children, once a week to the Sale Barn, the fanciest restaurant in town!

I learned so much about the ins-and-outs of working at a bank. Mr. Skola and his other secretaries treated me like their daughter. The hardest thing to learn was putting check copies under the correct last name. Kalona was a largely Amish community, so many of the last names were either Yoder or Miller. It was a problem for me because women often signed their checks simply as Mrs. Yoder or Mrs. Miller, using only their last name. Naturally, I was confused about who it was! The other secretaries would help me out with that since they knew everyone in town.

As fall neared, my parents and I decided that I should reconsider taking the teaching job in the fall. Mom and Dad felt strongly that I needed to go back to college in the fall, get my teaching credentials, and delay teaching until January. It was very difficult for me to tell the banker that, but the Board of Education was very understanding and let me out of my first teaching contract! Another valuable life experience!

As I approached my January graduation, I began looking again for a teaching job, and, amazingly, my roommate, Evelyn, and I were able to find jobs at the same school in the middle of the school year in Columbus Junction. The teachers were both expecting a baby, and were not planning to come back. Evelyn and I found an apartment, upstairs in Mr. and Mrs. Jones's home. It was small, but it had everything we needed, including our own kitchen. My parents donated a couch, but the rest was furnished. Perfect!

We were so excited to be starting out on our teaching adventure! My fifth-grade classroom had been relocated with the sixth-grade room, to the high school, out of space considerations, so I became good friends with my partner teacher in sixth grade. She was an experienced teacher who took me under her wing. Starting teaching in January turned out to be a blessing for me, since the teacher I was replacing left two weeks of plans, and had already set up a well-oiled routine of the class.

Evelyn Smith, on the left, and Donna Schueesler, who were roommates at Iowa State Teachers College, were both hired for their first teaching positions by the school board in Columbus Junction, Iowa, in December, 1953, to fill mid-year faculty vacancies in 3rd and 5th grades. Photo in Columbus Junction January 1954.

I had forty-two students in my class that first year, and I never gave it a thought, although I didn't have such a large class ever after that. They were, for the most part, so well behaved. There was only one class of each grade, and I was with my students from the moment they arrived at school until they left for the day, even eating lunch with them. You can imagine that I became very close to them, enjoying so many fun experiences together. I worked with the band teacher each year to put on a class program with every student participating in our little concert. As the year went on, some of the girls' parents asked if I would become a Girl Scout leader, and I jumped at the chance to have more fun with many of my students in the group!

This was my first teaching class(5th grade) in Columbus Junction. I'm in the back-nearly the same height as the kids!

My college years had given me much more than teaching credentials. I had learned that teaching was a good fit for me! I had learned to persevere in the face of health problems. I had learned that there are kind folks, some I barely knew, who were ready to give me a helping hand. I had learned the rewards of helping others with their challenges. I had learned that a disappointment can turn into a blessing later on. But more changes were on the horizon, as Don and I began making wedding plans.

PART 3

Young Adulthood
1955 - 1973

"There are only two lasting bequests we can hope to give our children. One of these is roots, the other, wings." Hodding Carter

My two miracle children that I hoped to give both roots and wings

Chapter 9
The Times

Women were beginning to spread their wings. With few exceptions, they still played a supporting role in American society, although that was ever-so-slowly changing. I got married in 1955 with the goal to become the best wife and mother that I could be. As an elementary school teacher, it seemed I could have the best of both worlds, a career and children. Society seemed to look upon teaching young children as a more appropriate career for a woman since it was a nurturing "motherly" role.

At the time, I never felt discriminated against because of my gender, although I was aware that becoming a school principal or superintendent of schools was reserved for men back then. That was fine with me since I didn't aspire to a position beyond a teaching job, which afforded me greater opportunity to properly care for children. I knew that teaching jobs were plentiful, so I reasoned that taking years off to raise children would not prevent me from finding another position much later. In addition, teachers followed the school calendar, so once my children started school, I could be there for them when they got home from school and in the summers.

Gone were the days when women were expected to give up their teaching career when they got married, but there were still other restrictions for female teachers. Dresses for women, not pants, was the only acceptable attire then. It wasn't until about 1970 that a woman was finally allowed to wear a "dressy" pant suit when teaching, but never jeans. In addition, small towns in Iowa didn't allow wives to teach in the same school district as their husbands.

It was becoming more acceptable for wives to work outside the home, I think partly because many women had been required to take over the jobs during WWII that had been previously filled by men who had gone to war. The Civil Rights Amendment in 1967 opened the door for women, when the word "sex" was added to "race, color, religion, or national origin" as being illegally discriminatory, but of course, people's attitudes and actions lagged behind the law.

Also of significance for women was the approval of the "pill" in 1960, with all of its ramifications for women's sexual liberation and the Women's Movement in general. Women gained the freedom to choose when and if, to become a mother. It was becoming more common for families to have two or three children rather than nine or ten! It seems to me that advances in feminine products allowed women a greater ability to participate fully in every aspect of life.

It didn't seem unusual to me at the time, but even car ownership was more a man's domain, as Detroit churned out those long, sleek, often two-toned cars, with the giant fenders of the late 50's. Many men also became experts at fixing and rebuilding their cars. I remember thinking my husband, Don, was crazy when he bought an old pickup truck for fifty dollars that didn't even run. It wasn't pretty like the car he drove every day, but Don installed the parts to get the truck running, all on his own!

I never had my own car until 1965, after my children were in school, and I had returned to teaching. It was an old black '55 Chevrolet, not one of those flashy late models! It makes me chuckle to think of that car. Don showed me a "magic lever" to push when the car would occasionally stall. Kindly folks would sometimes stop and offer help when they could see my car was giving me a problem, but I would just thank them and tell them that I was fine. I lifted the hood, pushed the lever, and was on my way. To this day, I don't know what that lever was, and with Don's passing a few years ago, it will remain a mystery!

Travel by train was still common, and I remember fondly the long-distance train trip in 1956 when Don and I went to the Rose Bowl in California where our beloved University of Iowa Hawkeye football team was playing. We probably wouldn't have been able to afford it, except for our dear friends, Mary Ann (Lorack) and Junior Burr, who invited us to stay with them since Junior had been assigned out there with the Navy. We had so much fun spending time with them!

Don and Mary Anne Burr in front of the Pasadena skyline-1956

We couldn't afford a sleeper car on the train, so we just reclined in our seats all night. We had even gotten permission from our regular mom-and-pop grocery store owner to forgo our monthly grocery tab so we would have enough money for the trip! The return trip was a little worrisome, as the train was running behind schedule, and we knew we would be cutting it close. We had to be home and teaching the morning we got back. So we ended up driving straight from the depot in Marion to our teaching jobs in Dysart, about an hour away!

As cars were becoming more reliable with fewer breakdowns and flat tires, cross-country road trips were becoming popular. Cars were also becoming faster, able to cruise at about 50 mph, but it wasn't until the 1960s that long distance travel could be maintained at the higher speeds. Roads were also improving, enabling a smoother ride at those faster speeds. In 1956, the Federal Aid Highway Act was approved, initiated by President Dwight Eisenhower's administration, creating our system of interstate highways with its unheard-of (at the time) speed limits. These are the highways we rely on today to get everywhere quickly!

Don's car in 1955

It wasn't until 1968 that all new American vehicles were required to have seat belts in their cars, but drivers and passengers were still not legally required to *wear* them. I remember that when they first appeared in cars, many folks didn't use them at all! Such "luxuries" as radios and air conditioners were now options you could pay for to add to the basic car you bought.

Commercial air travel was becoming more available to folks in the 1950s. I took my first commercial flight in 1958, when Don and I made a last-minute decision to join other University of Iowa football fans on a flight to cheer on our team at another Rose Bowl game in Pasadena, California. Only eleven years later, on July 20, 1969, Neil Armstrong walked on the moon. How far we'd come in such a short time!

World War II had united the American people in a common cause, but the 1960's ushered in a divisive time in our country. Civil Rights demonstrations, Vietnam War protests, LGBTQ activism, and women's marches punctuated the news. Although I was not an activist, I became keenly aware of the unrest when I attended the University of Iowa in the late '60s, when I made the decision to head back to school for a four-year teaching degree. I was attending my last semester of classes in order to graduate in June of 1970, when classes were disrupted by students blocking the doors to get into class buildings, protesting the Vietnam War.

It wasn't that I disagreed with their anti-war sentiments, but I desperately needed my class credits. I felt uncomfortable walking past them to go to class. Class attendance dwindled, so that at one point, there were only two other students still attending my Spanish class with me. Finally, university officials announced that we could keep the grade we had earned in class up to that point without attending further classes. And so it was that we ended that semester two weeks early.

While it was obvious that men had many opportunities that were not afforded women in that day, it was only men who were drafted into the Vietnam War which had begun in 1954. This gave women a certain advantage. As Americans became increasingly unhappy with that war, draft dodgers were making the news, some even leaving the country for Canada. I think it helped to lessen the divisive wounds of that war when President Jimmy Carter pardoned all Vietnam War draft dodgers in 1977.

Americans enjoyed new prosperity and an accompanying spending boom in the years following WW II, ushering in the new concept of credit cards. Credit had been available in the form of bank loans, and for smaller purchases, store credit, but it wasn't until the 1950s when the Diner's Club launched the first credit card.

I never had a credit card until 1957 when Don and I got one after we were told by the bank that we needed one to have a credit history in order to buy our first home. I remember that my card was in Don's name, since the first credit cards were issued in the husband's name only. Again, that's just the way it was, so I didn't think much about it at the time.

Written communication had been revolutionized with the invention of the typewriter, which had come into wide-spread use around 1915, with its loud clickity clackity sound. Constant improvements were made to make it quieter and less likely to jam, but it wasn't until the 1960s that the electric typewriter came on the scene.

I had my first experience using an electric typewriter around 1970, when Mom bought one to assist her in writing her book on genealogy. Although she had never learned to type herself, she hired a woman to type for her. Ultimately, I did much of the typing, with the assistance of my daughter, Diane, who at that time was just a sophomore in high school.

We had no idea then of the transformation that was just around the corner with the coming of the personal computer! In 1971, I became aware of computers when the schools began to get some. We teachers took computer classes to help introduce computer skills to students, and later, we were able to purchase our own home computer. The beginning of a new world in communication!

The microwave oven had also been invented, and in 1962, we got one of these amazing appliances that could heat food up almost instantaneously! Soon after, answering machines for telephones became available. Suddenly you didn't have to be home to get messages, and you could screen your calls as well! I think that microwaves, answering machines, and the computer were the inventions that changed our lives the most at that time.

Chapter 10
Wedding Bells

Our wedding day-May 27, 1955

I felt like a fairytale princess on the day of my wedding! I was twenty-one years old when I married Donald James Bean on May 27, 1955, a young man I had met on my one and only blind date. You never know where a chance happening will lead! But how could I know that Don was "the one", because marriage, in my mind, was forever? It was one of the rare times that I remember going to Mom about something so personal. She seemed to know just the right questions to ask me about how he treated me, financial considerations, the way we worked through disagreements, similar interests, and common goals.

Like me, Don had grown up on an Iowa farm and was a teacher. He was so level-headed and nothing seemed to upset him. He knew how to repair and build anything. We seemed to think alike in so many ways, having shared values. I knew I could trust him with my life. Everything felt so right! Looking back over our many years together, we had our ups and downs, but we were both committed to working things out with each other.

My sister, Joyce, recalls that, before she got married in 1968, Joanne and I (by then "old" married ladies) took her aside to tell her that "there comes a time in the best of marriages, when you may want out, but just remember that it is normal to have such feelings. That time will pass." I think that was the key to our sixty-two years of marriage. Although there came a time when I admit that I felt that way myself, Don and I were able to work through it, committed to our relationship and to meeting challenges together.

I was thrilled when Don made it official with my beautiful engagement ring. It was perfect in every way, although it was a little too large at first. I had to keep it from falling off my ring finger by holding it with my thumb. We were attending a high school basketball game that night, so I got to show my ring off to everyone there. I was determined to wear it teaching the next day and not let it fall off before I could get the size adjusted!

Joanne and Marvin, being two and four years older than me, had both had traditional ceremonies, which is how I wanted mine to be. Don and I were married at my family's church, the Evangelical and Reformed Church in Lone Tree. The church was almost dream-like to me, so beautifully decorated by my mother and the church ladies with purple and white flowers! It was an evening candlelit service, with Terry Edmonds, Don's much younger cousin, serving as candlelighter before the service began. He ceremoniously lit candles in the windows around the sanctuary, ending with the candelabra on the chancel, setting a lovely mood.

The wedding party was small, with family and close friends attending Don and me. The women and girls were all in purple dresses, handsewn by my mother. Always frugal, I wore Joanne's wedding dress, making some minor sewing adjustments to fit my smaller size. Joanne, who was my maid of honor, and I dressed at the minister's parsonage next door to the church. Mr. Bowen, the photographer, even took pictures of us there just before the ceremony.

From left: Maynard Edmonds,Marvin, Joyce, Joanne, Donna, Don, Richard Bean, Terry Edmonds, Kenny Powers, Junior Burr
In front, Tommy Heither and Cheryl Schuessler

Dad, Mom, Me, Don, Dorothy and James Bean

The idea of having a sit-down dinner after a wedding was unheard of to me. Our reception was held in the church basement with cake, ice cream, nuts, mints, coffee, and punch. After refreshments, we opened our wedding presents in front of everyone. We were so grateful for the many gifts from family and friends, but I was especially delighted to receive a lovely porcelain cream and sugar set given by my fifth-grade students. They had collected money to purchase the set, and with thirty-one cents left over, they put thirty-one pennies inside the sugar bowl, which I still have to this day, pennies included! They told me that was so I would never be broke!

All went smoothly that day, but not everything was perfect. I had a history of spring throat infections, and ended up going to Dr. Jacques (also a guest at our wedding) that very morning! He gave me a strong antibiotic that had to be taken with milk, so I would feel well enough to enjoy the day's events. Thankfully, I did!

Don's brand new car and our honeymoon outfits

We began our honeymoon directly after the reception, leaving about 9:30 pm for St. Louis. Although Don didn't have much money then, he had saved up to purchase a beautiful new 1955 maroon and white Chevrolet. I had never even ridden in it before! Don had a "thing" about his cars, always keeping them pristine. I think his car was his haven! I remember that when we were first married, he asked that I not lean my head against the window of his car as it might leave a grease mark!

The honeymoon trip was going well until it was time to take my throat medication, and I realized that I had forgotten to bring the milk to take it. Don pulled into a little gas station to purchase some milk (fast food chains were not around yet), but they didn't sell small size cartons. Instead, they poured milk from a gallon jug (already opened) into an empty milk carton, leaving the top open so I could drink from it. But why not a paper cup, you ask? They weren't yet in general use!

I was trying to be so careful not to spill it, so I pushed the top down on the carton to close it. In the process, I squirted milk all over my special "going-away" dress and Don's new car! I was beside myself as I tried to clean it up as best I could, knowing Don must have been frantic about his car! But he never said a word.

We had to drive late into the night to find a motel since it was Memorial Day weekend. Overall, our honeymoon turned out beautifully, seeing a St. Louis Cardinal baseball game and touring the city, but we couldn't find our car in the lot after we visited the St. Louis Zoo. As it often happens, neither of us had paid much attention to where we had parked in the zoo parking lot. It seemed like hours that we kept walking around trying to find our car and it kept getting darker, until we remembered that we had parked near a flower garden. We asked an attendant, who quickly directed us to the flower garden!

When we were leaving St. Louis, I was pleasantly surprised when Don asked if I wanted to drive his new car. I proudly approached a busy intersection going out of the city, when in the middle of the intersection, the car died! It was a stick shift and I wasn't so experienced with that. I finally got it into the correct gear and made it through without incident. Don didn't seem annoyed, but he quickly offered to drive after that!

Don and I felt lucky to have both gotten a junior high teaching job in the friendly little town of Dysart, Iowa, because at the time, a husband and wife were often not allowed to teach in the same district, especially in the smaller towns. Dysart was the perfect place for us to start out our married life, with its kind people, enough stores for what we might need, a great school, and a Methodist church. Of course, I soon became involved with the church women's activities and joined the choir, singing lots of solos.

I was hired to teach sixth grade, but Don had longer days, teaching junior high science, coaching boys' football, and driving a school bus before and after school. Without much money, and being young and energetic, we looked for ways to get by. In those early years of our marriage, we kept a jar in the house, where we each put our loose change at the end of the day. It was a little "insurance" money that we only dipped into if things got tight at the end of the month. Several times that jar got us through to the next pay day!

When we first moved to Dysart, we rented a second story apartment, but at the end of our second year, we purchased our first home there from the science teacher. It was an older home that needed work, so it didn't cost so much. We had never had a credit card and thus had no credit rating, so my parents loaned us the $3000 to pay for the house. The house had no furnace, just a large oil-burning pot belly stove in the living room. The upstairs had no heat except what drifted up through the floor registers.

That summer, we sublet an apartment in Iowa City so that Don could work on his Master's Degree at the University of Iowa, driving to Dysart every weekend to work on our house there. Don put in new windows, cupboards, and even new plumbing. The store, where we purchased our supplies, wanted to hire Don to work for them when they saw his beautiful work! Don's dad stayed with us two weeks while he and Don turned a small outbuilding on the property into a one stall garage.

The teachers at our school became our best friends, like Mark Poggemiller, who taught with Don, and came for dinner at our house about once a week. Another teacher, Sylvia Heckroth, became like a mother to me, sharing her ideas, and taking me under her wing. Our third year in Dysart, the school decided to move my sixth-grade class into the Junior High with the seventh and eighth grade classes, so I began teaching Language Arts. We taught from carts, moving from room to room. I admit I was worried about teaching the older students, but it all went well.

That same year, I was ecstatic to learn that I was going to be mother! I kept it quiet for a while, but it didn't stay a secret very long because the junior high girls noticed that I could not zipper my skirt under my jacket one day when I bent over.

They also noticed that I was now buying milk with my lunches at school, and I had never done that before!

Early one spring morning, when I was about seven and a half months pregnant, Don dropped me off at school on his way to begin his morning bus route. I usually walked to school, but I had a desk full of papers that needed to be corrected so I wanted to get there early. As I dashed up the stairs to my room, I felt (and saw) a rush of blood coming down my leg, and then a pain in my stomach.

I immediately called my doctor and he told me to meet him in his office. I quickly walked there, not knowing what was wrong. Walking was probably not what he had in mind! He told me that I was in labor and that I needed to have someone drive me home and go straight to bed. I was in shock! I called my teacher friend, Sylvia, and she took care of everything, driving me home, putting me to bed, and calling the school to get a substitute teacher for my class. I was so scared, not knowing what was happening!

When Don arrived at school, they told him my news. I called my parents and they came to stay with me for a few days, while I was bed-ridden. Gradually the pain subsided and the blood became less. After two weeks in bed, the doctor gave me the OK to return to school, but I had to do everything very slowly for the duration of my pregnancy.

After school was out, Don took up college courses again to finish up his Master's Degree in Iowa City, commuting with two of his friends. It was at this time that the state of Iowa decided to allow each town to decide whether or not they would go on Daylight Savings Time. You can imagine the confusion and inconvenience it caused whenever you traveled from one town to another! So, when Don and his friends drove to Iowa City for classes, they had to leave at 5AM from Dysart for their 7AM class in Iowa City (which was 6AM in Dysart time)!

On the morning of July 16 (two weeks after my due date), as Don was getting ready to meet his friends to head for Iowa City, my labor pains began. But instead of going to class that day, Don ended up taking me straight to the hospital in Waterloo, about forty-five minutes away, calling the doctor to have him meet us there. I was in hard labor until 10:30 that night, in and out of the delivery room three times! The doctor could see the baby's head, but she couldn't be born until he finally decided to turn her.

The doctor told me he would save me, but was not sure if he could also save the baby. In those days, husbands were not allowed in the delivery room, so I was on my own with the doctor. A most frightening time in my life! At 10:30 PM, Diane Renee was born with slight yellow jaundice, several birth marks, and instrument bruises, but to me, she was perfect and beautiful! Our miracle baby was born!

Don and I decided that, even with our limited means, it was important that I stay home to be a full-time mom for our baby. Don was able to get a higher paying teaching job in the big city of Cedar Rapids, so in 1958, we moved there for him to teach physical education at the brand-new Wright Elementary School. Our home in Dysart sold right away. The buyers literally moved in through the back door, the same day we moved out through the front door!

 We could not find (or afford!) a moving company to move us since it was Memorial Day weekend. A good friend who shipped livestock in his huge truck said he would clean out his semi and help us move. And so it was that we moved to our little three-bedroom ranch home, close to Don's school in Cedar Rapids. It had no basement, but it had a large utility room, a large single garage, and a fenced-in back yard. It seemed just right for our new family!

Don loved his job at Wright School, enjoying his fellow teachers. I was happy to be home to care for Diane. We still had only one car, but I didn't feel so isolated since our church and a small shopping mall were close enough that I could take Diane on long walks to both. I did some occasional substitute teaching, mostly at Wright School, so both Don and I developed friendships there.

Don doing one of his favorite things-Golf!

Don loved living so close to several golf courses, playing many days throughout the summer. When the temperature was ninety degrees, I would ask how he could play golf, but his reply was "There is always a breeze on the golf course!". We were also happy that living in Cedar Rapids meant that our parents and relatives lived closer and we could see them more often.

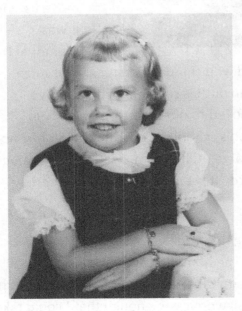

About a year after our move to Cedar Rapids, I was delighted to find out that I was going to be a mother again! My new doctor knew my difficult history, and that it was natural for me to be concerned when I was again two weeks late. Don's mother came to stay with Diane while I had the baby. On October 17, 1959, I woke at 2:30 AM with abdominal pains. Don remembered the long day of waiting it had been when Diane was born, so he was in no rush to get to the hospital.

100

But I knew differently, so I told him to drive as fast as he could and if a policeman stopped us, to have him lead us to the hospital. Don continued his normal pace until I told him I thought I was having this baby in the car! When we arrived at the hospital, they were outside with a wheel chair for me. I told them to please hurry as they wheeled me in.

Don parked the car, and by the time he got to the baby ward, they told him he had a baby girl, DeLana Kay! He was back home in bed within an hour of leaving the house! Everything had gone well and very quickly. We were so happy to have two special little girls! Diane was two years old and adored her baby sister, helping with little errands whenever she could.

DeLana's birth had gone smoothly (and so quickly!), but she had a difficult time of it with colic for the first six months of her life. That meant she cried, really screamed, so much of the time, and we couldn't find anything that would help her. It became difficult for me to even think of going anywhere with her, even to see relatives, who always had the "perfect" advice for me! Fortunately, it all ended as suddenly as it had appeared when DeLana turned six months old, like magic!

It was in my early years of marriage that I had some doubts and began to consider the direction of my life. I'd led a pretty carefree life up to then, pursuing my own interests with my parents always looking out for me. Sharing everything in life and having to include someone else in every important decision was a big adjustment for me. I was very happy most of the time, but at other times, I couldn't help thinking of how it was when I was single and fancy-free.

101

In the end, I came to realize that Don was the best thing that ever happened to me. He was kind, patient, loving, and even-tempered. He was five years older and more mature than I was. Don and I talked through what responsibilities we would share and what things we would not, beginning with setting up individual bank accounts and checkbooks, dividing household expenses down the middle. That plan worked for both us throughout our marriage.

We also considered how we could maintain our individuality within the togetherness of marriage. We ultimately agreed that it was important for us to maintain our independent activities, but just as important to cultivate the things we loved to do together. Don loved golf, bowling, and all sports, and got tremendous satisfaction from his work with the Army Reserves. I was interested in singing, church, and sewing.

Together, we had great times getting together with friends playing "500" (a favorite card game), attending school and church activities, and of course, dancing, especially at the elegant Armar Ballroom in Cedar Rapids. It was THE place to be at that time, with its rotating mirrored ball hanging from the ceiling, while we danced to the best bands around, like Tommy Dorsey, Guy Lombardo, and Wayne King. It was said it could hold 3,000 people with seating around the edges of the floor for 1,500!

And so it was that my married life began, coming to understand that we needed both time on our own as well as time together for our happiness. I'm reminded of the following quote from Khalil Gibran, whose wise words I learned about only many years later.

"Love one another but make not a bond of love.
Let it rather be a moving sea between the shores of your souls.
Fill each other's cup but drink not from one cup.
Give one another of your bread but eat not from the same loaf.
Sing and dance together and be joyous, but let each one of you be alone, even as the strings of a lute are alone though they quiver with the same music.
Give your hearts, but not into each other's keeping.
For only the hand of Life can contain your hearts.
And stand together, yet not too near together:
For the pillars of the temple stand apart,
And the oak tree and the cypress grow not in each other's shadow."
— Khalil Gibran, The Prophet

Chapter 11
Shifting Priorities

I think becoming a mother really propelled me into adulthood, when my own priorities took a back seat to the needs of my little daughters, Diane and DeLana. It was important to me to put my teaching on hold so I could stay at home with my girls. I'd always had a strong connection to little ones, starting with my baby sister, Joyce (thirteen years younger than I am), my babysitting years throughout high school, and my teaching experience with elementary school children.

Diane, 4, DeLana 1 ½- 1961

Don and I could see that we needed a bigger home for our family, and we wanted to be settled there before Diane started Kindergarten. We couldn't find a house in our price range that would work, but we found an empty lot in a developing housing area in nearby Marion. We talked to a builder that would allow Don and I to do much of the work on the house as a down payment. Once we moved into our house in Marion, we rented our house in Cedar Rapids for extra income.

Don and I did all the painting, finished all the woodwork, graded the yard, and anything else that had to be done in our new house, although we probably wouldn't have qualified for a Certificate of Occupancy in today's world when we moved in! The house still needed so much work, but it was livable enough for us while we finished things off. At that time, the area with our lot was on the edge of Marion, next to some cornfields with a few houses nearby.

Our home was literally out in the dusty (or muddy!) cornfields! For several years, we watched farmers work in their fields behind the house. Don had put in a patio and a swing set for the girls, although we didn't have a grassy lawn yet, just mostly dirt in our backyard. One day after it had rained, little Diane, not more than three years old, went out to swing and got stuck in the thick mud. I was sitting on the patio when I heard her yell, "Help me! Help me!"

I guess we were so proud of our new home that we wanted to host Thanksgiving dinner for the family (about twelve people) soon after we moved in. Little did we know that the water would be turned on only three days before Thanksgiving Day! The stove was not yet hooked up so a neighbor kindly offered to cook the turkey for us!

The city of Marion didn't pay much attention to our sparsely populated area on the outskirts of town. We had to pick up our mail at the end of our long, uphill block, near the new elementary school. Snow plows got to our area of town last, so that on snowy days, Don had to assess how he was going to get out to go to school since they often hadn't plowed our street yet. Sometimes it was clear enough to go down the driveway to the street, but often he just cut across the field! If someone came by our house later, I would look out the window to see which way Don had gotten through the snow, and tell them to "follow his tracks"!

During these years, I was content to be a stay-at-home mom, but teaching was never out of my mind. The summer before Diane started Kindergarten, I got a call from the nearby Starry Elementary School PTA to ask if I would be next year's PTA president. It seemed a little strange to me, since I had no child in school at the time, but I thought that it would be a good way to get acquainted with the people in the area. The school was so close, I could even walk there, since we still only had one car at the time. Thus it was that my connection to education was renewed!

My involvement in the PTA soon grew into much more, as I became the volunteer person to do almost anything, including helping out in the school office, and eventually I became a substitute teacher there for a number of years. I remember that when Diane saw me when I substituted at her school, she was always so happy to see me, but when DeLana saw me there, she never looked my way, like she didn't know who I was! The girls were alike in some ways, but so different in others!

Diane loved being a big sister, always looking out for DeLana, while DeLana always looked up to Diane, paying close attention to whatever Diane did, and making sure she didn't repeat anything that would get her in trouble! DeLana was so often Don's shadow, in the middle of whatever project he was working on. She even asked for a toolbox from Santa one year. Diane, on the other hand, liked to be by my side, helping with whatever I was doing.

Both girls were like little mothers with our animals, taking either one of our rabbits or our miniature terrier dog in their doll strollers for walks outside. They also both helped with our huge garden, watching the plants mature and eating the fresh vegetables right off the vine. Barbies had become the rage for little girls, and Diane and DeLana were no exception. I think Barbies took the place of my beloved childhood paper dolls.

I gave beginning piano lessons to both our girls, and also to my hairdresser's son, Lawson. Lawson's mom set my long hair into a French twist every week and I gave him a piano lesson every week, so no pay was involved! I was in heaven! I have always disliked doing anything with my hair! Don did not even complain when I went to bed each night with toilet paper wrapped around my head with a hair net to hold it all on so the "do" would last a longer time!

Diane was often "glued" to a book, from the time she first started reading. At times Diane would tune us out because she was so engrossed in whatever book she was reading, and all the while, she remembered the details of the story perfectly. Can you imagine telling your child to "Put that book down!"? It was no surprise that Diane grew up to become a respected reading teacher in our area, continuing her active involvement on the Board of the Iowa Reading Association, even after she retired from teaching!

Don and I were fortunate to have such sweet, good-natured daughters, even when they were small. We had few surprises with Diane, but DeLana had definite ideas about most everything! When DeLana began Kindergarten, she would only wear dresses that fell below her knees. Much later, when I asked her about that, she explained that she thought she was too fat to show her knees!

When DeLana was a bit older (when Don and I were both teaching), she asked if she could walk home for lunch every day (by herself). I finally agreed, only to find out some time later (to my surprise!) that she had decided to put herself on a "dill-pickle-only lunch diet", in order to lose weight! She was certainly not obese, but she was a little chubby, and she came up with her own way of doing something about it!

From an early age, DeLana had a gift for anything artistic. When she was around six years old, she used my scrap fabric and cut out clothes for her dolls. She never used a pattern. She just cut: snip, snip, snip and she was done! It always fit! She seemed to notice everything about everything! Even when she was very young, DeLana would talk about the color or design of people's clothes, shoes or room colors, of somewhere we had been. It's no wonder that she became one of Cedar Rapids best art teachers!

I suppose it was natural that both Diane and DeLana had "teacher blood" in them. When Diane was about twelve, she began doing short daytime babysitting jobs, and soon our home became a gathering place for the kids in our growing neighborhood. Diane and DeLana were the oldest children in the neighborhood, so they began to organize activities for the others. As time went on, the activities became more formalized, when Diane and DeLana organized a "summer school" for all the neighbor children. They took turns being the teacher, planning the classes every day, including recess and snack time. At the end of summer, they even held a graduation ceremony complete with homemade graduation hats, inviting all the parents!

Diane had been our miracle baby at birth, but DeLana had so many childhood health issues that she became our second miracle child! It seemed she cried constantly as a baby from a severe case of colic until she was six months old. At around two months old, we noticed that her legs were not developing correctly, both pointing the same direction. The doctor showed Don how to make a wooden foot brace which DeLana wore whenever she was in her crib, until she was two years old. She got pretty good at getting around the edge of her crib with the brace on!

When DeLana was about four, she began having ear infections, one after the other, that medication didn't touch. She ended up having both her tonsils and adenoids removed then. Soon after, she began having unexplained nose bleeds, as often as once a week, tapering off around her junior high years. I remember Don having similar nose bleeds as an adult, which ended about the time he became a regular blood donor.

Diane caused a scare of her own when we had to rush her to the hospital for a badly broken arm. It was Diane's last day of sixth grade and we were celebrating at a neighbor's house. The kids were excited to go outside to jump on their trampoline. Now, Diane liked jumping on the trampoline since Don had taken the girls many times to his school gymnasium, so when the kids asked Diane to do a flip, she was happy to oblige. The only problem was that she had never actually tried one!

Not surprisingly, she didn't complete the full flip and landed on her right arm, her dominant arm! The break was so bad, she looked like she had two elbows! The doctors tried to reset the arm twice, without success. They ended up putting a steel rod in her arm with a cast from her elbow to her wrist. Her cast and rod were removed the day before Diane started seventh grade, but it took the rest of the school year to fully heal. A doctor's note allowed her to be exempt from full participation in gym activities, becoming the gym teacher's assistant and eventually good friend.

Having a picnic by a mountain stream on our vacation out West with Diane's broken arm- 1970.

I admit that there were times when I felt like a failure as a mother, like the morning the girls and I had just returned from the store. I was busy unloading bags onto the kitchen table, while the girls were playing doctor. I had just gotten a new bottle of children's vitamins in my purchases, the colorful animal-shaped fruit flavored kind that was common back then, so enticing to children. I began fixing lunch, when I noticed that the vitamin bottle was open and that it was not full.

DeLana was only about two years old at the time, and I suppose she thought the vitamins would make good pills for playing doctor. When I realized what must have happened, I immediately called the doctor who said to bring DeLana right in to pump her stomach! When I arrived at the hospital, the doctor grabbed DeLana out of my arms and took her into another room.

When they brought her back out to me, her face was white and covered with red dots. The doctor said she had cried so hard that she broke a few blood vessels, but that the red spots would soon disappear. I felt like I had been such a bad, neglectful mother! It didn't help when the new-to-me doctor yelled at me and berated my abilities as a mother! I vowed to be more careful about such things in the future!

When Diane was about five, she got a "glacier" of solid red all over her body, which turned out to be measles with no spots. At the time, DeLana had just recovered from mumps, so we were naturally concerned that Diane would have mumps with her measles! Fortunately, Diane must be immune to mumps because she has never had them to this day!

I received my life's major blow about this time, in 1964, when I found out that the arrival of our third child was not to be. Don and I had planned it out carefully, but when I was almost eight months along in my pregnancy, the doctor discovered the fetus was not alive. Unfortunately, Don was away at his regular two-week summer camp for the Army Reserves when I got the news. I was beside myself with grief, and without cell phones in those days, I wasn't able to get hold of Don to even let him know.

Through my tears, I tried to call Mom and Dad with the terrible news, but my dear neighbor, June, came over and made the call for me. I needed someone to stay with Diane and DeLana while I was in the hospital, but Mom and Dad were in the midst of farm work, so they brought my sister, Joyce, now in high school, to take care of the girls. Joyce always was so good with our girls, and they always had fun times with her, so I had no worries.

By the time Don returned home from Army Reserve camp, I was home from the hospital. I had learned that I could not have any more children. Don and I were devastated with our loss, but it was a particularly difficult time for me as I would have bouts of unexpectedly breaking into tears.

I avoided seeing people I knew, because when they saw that I was no longer pregnant, they assumed I had had the baby and would offer their congratulations. More tears! It got so bad that I didn't want to leave the house, but Don was so patient and caring. Without him, I don't know how I would have gotten out of my depression. Something so terrible had brought us closer together.

Don and I made enduring friendships during our time at our house in Marion, like our neighbors Don and Shirley Turecek, who also had two children at the time. We met LaVonn and Roger (Bud) Messerly through the school where Bud was the principal. Don and Bud shared a love for golf and Iowa Hawkeye football, so the four of us attended most Iowa football games. LaVonn taught me how to knit and quilt. We

began having monthly Bridge parties, adding Jean and Bill Lynch to our circle of friends as well as Walt and Pat Scott.

Donna with friends, LaVonn and Roger (Bud) Messerly

Don and Shirley Turecek with Don and I

That group of young parents was an important support group for Don and me during these years of figuring out parenting. We had such wonderful family times with Diane and DeLana, but I think we got through the challenging situations because Don and I were both devoted to our little girls and to each other!

113

Jean and Bill Lynch were also good friends of ours. Jean was the secretary at Wright School. When they retired, they moved to Lake of the Ozarks where we visited them often.

Genny Kedrovsky was a friend who taught at Wright with Don. She loved kids and visited often. When she came to visit in the evening she would tuck in the girls and read them a bedtime story.

All of the people in the above pictures are (or were) lifelong friends.

When both girls were in school, an opportunity arose for me to go back to full time teaching in Cedar Rapids. Wright School, where Don was teaching, needed a first-grade teacher, and since I had been doing substitute teaching there, the principal asked me if I was interested. I told him "I wasn't sure that I was cut out to teach first grade", which was probably not the best way for me to get a job! But Mr. Snyder reassured me, saying "I know you can do it".

Don and the girls encouraged me to take the job, telling me that I was "easier to be around" when I was teaching. I knew that another regular income would make our lives easier. In the end, I loved the job, beginning my special connection with first graders.

While I was teaching, I began taking college night classes and summer classes to work towards a four-year BA degree in teaching, which was becoming the norm. I had earned about one year of credits when I decided to simply take a year's break from teaching to pursue courses to that end at the University of Iowa in Iowa City, over an hour away. I knew it would not be easy, but I didn't realize it at the time, that the experience would cause me to question why I had ever begun such a difficult undertaking!

The university required me to take two years of a foreign language, which I had not had previously. I was determined to get the courses I needed in as short a time as possible. While I took First Semester Spanish at Iowa during the day, I took Second Semester Spanish at night at Coe College! I enrolled in my second year of Spanish the following summer at Mount Mercy College. I think that's what is called "burning the candle at both ends"! It almost proved my undoing.

I told no one of my Spanish plan except Mr. Almazov, who taught Spanish at Coe College. I had a long talk with him about my concerns, and he assured me that I would be able to do it because I was so driven. However, after two weeks of my Spanish marathon of classes, I told Mr. Almazov that I did not know any Spanish words in his night class and that I didn't think I could manage it all!

Dear Mr. Almazov said he was willing to give me extra help if I could come a half hour early to every one of his classes. It worked! Both my day and evening classes were becoming easier, and I passed both! Mr. Almazov also took the time and patience to prepare me for my second year of Spanish the following summer at Mount Mercy College. I was overwhelmed by his kindness and the faith he had in me!

And so it was that only with Mr. Almazov's help, I completed two years of Spanish in seven months! He would not accept any money or gift that I tried to give him for getting me through Spanish. There is no way I can ever thank him adequately for what he did. Truly, one of my guardian angels!

Throughout this time, I ate, drank, and slept Spanish. Diane was a huge help to me, reading parts of the Spanish lesson to me to help me memorize my part every day, even though she didn't know Spanish herself. Every class required me to speak only Spanish in class, so the pressure was on! Altogether I lost twenty-four pounds from my five-foot-five frame, weighing only one hundred pounds by the time I was done with Spanish classes!

It is an understatement to say that these college years were challenging, but in the end, I learned how to persevere through difficult times, how to accomplish things I never thought I could, and how wonderful people can be. I know Don and the girls were overjoyed to have me be done with that experience, but I could not have done it without their loving help and patience!

Coincidentally, Joyce had graduated high school and was attending the University at the same time I began taking classes there. When it came time for me to register for my

116

classes, Joyce suggested that she accompany me. I told her she didn't need to bother since I knew I could figure it out. Joyce explained that the first time she had registered, she was in tears before she finished!

Registration was very different back then. There were 20,000 students at Iowa, and registration was all done with face-to-face signups on paper, nothing online, so you can imagine the hubbub of craziness at the Field House where it was held! The most frustrating part was getting in line to sign up for a class you needed, only to find it was full when you got to the table at the front of the line, and then having to rework your schedule on the spot in order to have the classes you needed to graduate!

Joyce and I had never attended school of any kind together because of our age difference, so it was a special time. We arranged to meet for lunch at the Memorial Union on campus once a week! It was also during this time that Mom took a job as a cook at one of the sororities so I stopped by once a week to see her, often helping her prepare food. It was a wonderful bonding time with both Mom and Joyce!

And so it was that I had gotten married, had two daughters, completed a four-year BA degree in teaching, and returned to full-time teaching, all within a span of a few years. I couldn't imagine what more life could have in store for me!

DeLana,4, Don and Diane,6, ready for Easter Sunday

Chapter 12
Special Times

Suddenly there were eight little cousins as Marvin, Joanne, and I all had children within a few years of each other. There were fewer visits to my aunts and uncles then, because we had all become aunts and uncles ourselves, and Mom and Dad had become proud grandparents to eight children all around the same age! Their farm became the gathering place for our three growing families.

My younger sister, Joyce, who was still in high school at this time, was like a big sister to all her new nieces and one nephew. As Joyce recalls it, "I couldn't get enough of them, playing games, pushing them on the big tree swing, or roping them into some newly concocted play which they presented to the adults". When the cousins got a bit older, they built a tree house out back of the farmhouse and organized their own club, even sewing a flag to represent it. Fun times!

The Dating Game-one of the many plays with the Hopton cousins

Terri, Diane, Greg and DeLana in 2023 with the club flag that DeLana made as a child

Marvin and Pat's Wedding-I'm beside Pat and Joyce is in front of Marvin.

Marvin had married Pat Hogan, in my eyes a glamorous city girl from Iowa City, so pretty with deep dimples. They had three daughters, Cheryl, Karen, and Cynthia. Being the only boy in our family, Marvin had always been more than a son to Dad. He'd been his soulmate and friend, by Dad's side throughout his life, becoming a farmer himself, eventually taking over our Uncle Albert's farm, after he retired and moved to Iowa City. That farm was adjacent to Dad's farm, so they continued farming side by side.

Marvin's wife, Pat, had not grown up on a farm, and wasn't so familiar with farm life. She and Marvin made a good team in many ways, but I never felt that Pat had an easy time of it trying to fit into our farm family. It was obvious she was a wonderful mother and homemaker, but it seemed to me that her outlook was not in sync with that of the typical farmwife back then. While she joined Marvin working in the garden, and even canning vegetables, she was not often seen at Marvin's side helping with the crop work. Mom's disapproval could be felt when she noticed that Pat did not sew her children's clothes, or that she dared to hang out laundry on a Sunday!

Joanne and Rick's Wedding-I'm beside Joanne and Joyce is in front of her.

Joanne married Freddie Wayne Hopton, introduced to us Iowa folks as "Rick", but Joanne explained that he was "Fred" to his coworkers at General Electric and "Wayne" to family and friends where he grew up in Ohio. He and Joanne met while he was in the Air Force, and the military decided his legal name was Frederick, not Freddie, and so his Air Force buddies all called him Rick. It was during this time that we Iowa relatives met him, so he was always Rick to us! They soon had three children, Pam, Greg, and Terri. Greg was the only boy in an abundance of girl cousins! Joanne cut short her teaching career to be a full-time mom, adding sons Brad and Brian some years later, making five Hopton children altogether.

Terri, Brad, Rick, Greg, Joanne, Brian and Pam Hopton-1978

Unlike Don, Rick did not grow up on a farm, and worked for General Electric in Cincinnati. Rick was a smoker when they were first married, which I know Mom did not approve of. Nevertheless, she dutifully brought out her one and only ashtray whenever they came for a visit. I believe Rick was able to fit into our family for two reasons. The first is that he impressed Mom because he was from a church-going family, very involved in the Church of Christ, regularly attending Sunday services. I remember that whenever they visited from Ohio, Mom was happy that Rick offered a blessing before every meal, which had never been our custom.

I think that Rick was comfortable in our family also because he found an ally in Don. The two of them hit it off from the start, sharing a love for the new streamlined cars, bowling, and especially golf. They were both easy going and fun-loving.

121

Rick and Don had a running rivalry, all the years they knew each other, about their favorite football teams. They could often be heard teasing about how much better the Iowa Hawkeyes were than the Ohio Buckeyes, and vice versa! Even the little kids got into it, coached by their dads, yelling "Yay Hawkeyes!" or "Yay Buckeyes!".

On one occasion, Rick bought tickets to an Iowa/Ohio football game in Cincinnati, whereupon Don and one of his Iowa buddies, his principal Keith Wymore, traveled to Ohio to see the game with Rick. Don and Keith had Hawkeye sweatshirts to wear, so Don brought one for Rick. To everyone's amazement, Rick actually wore the sweatshirt to the game, so they were a sight to see, sitting in the stands in the Ohio section. You can imagine the hard time the Ohioans gave these Iowa fans sitting in their midst, but Rick never blinked an eye!

Don's five-years-younger brother, Richard, married Carol Conklin in 1957, shortly after we got married, in a small church wedding with Don and I attending them. They eventually bought a house in Ainsworth, a small town not far from Lone Tree, where they lived their entire married lives. Carol was an elementary school teacher so we shared an important focus in our lives. They had three children, Doug, Angie, and Jeff, who were around the same age as Diane and DeLana, so it was fun to get together as young parents.

Richard had a more reserved personality than Don, though it was obvious they enjoyed their times together. Although Richard wasn't "into" sports like Don, his children were involved in different ways. Doug became a sports writer for a newspaper. Angie was the star pitcher on her high school softball team. Jeff became quite a golfer, and in later years,

often partnered with Don on the links. Over the years, the two developed a strong bond, almost like father-son.

Don and Richard's parents, James (or Jim as he like to be called) and Dorothy Wall Bean, were very involved in their children's and grandchildren's lives.

Dorothy had been a country school teacher her entire life, so she was a natural to step in to care for any of our children whenever she was needed. Dorothy was famous for her cooking, especially her cherry pies, cinnamon rolls, and other tasty desserts. She made her own homemade noodles, like Mom.

Dorothy was also a talented seamstress and crocheted many beautiful doilies! She was a wonderful grandma, but she could be outspoken with her advice, especially for her daughters-in-law, so Carol and I learned to take it all with a grain of salt!

Don's dad, Jim, was a gentle soul, with a personality much like Don's. Nothing seemed to bother him, and I don't ever recall

123

hearing him raise his voice. He had been a life-long farmer, and he could build or repair most anything, always ready to lend a hand. I recall that he let Dorothy do most of the talking in the family, but you knew to listen when he spoke up.

Edith and Art with all of their children at their 50th anniversary

My parents, Edith and Arthur Schuessler, now grandparents of eight (Brad, Brian and Carolyn came much later), especially delighted in having all of them together which happened whenever Hoptons came from Ohio for summer stays at the farm. They even rented a pony for the grandchildren to ride while everyone was there. Such fun they all had!

In later years, with the grandchildren growing up and their lives quieting down, Mom became more and more interested in genealogy, with Dad joining her on excursions to old cemeteries and genealogical libraries around the country where she would take copious notes. Dad told me once that he sometimes found her at the table writing, far into the night. In 1979, she authored and published a book "Pioneers and Their Descendants of the Lone Tree Area", a book of over a thousand pages!

Dad was content in his later years keeping notebooks of his favorite jokes and delighting everyone whenever we came around! Surprisingly, he showed a different side of himself as he came to love making ceramics, creating figurines, teapots, and even several beautiful manger scenes, so removed from his life's work on the farm!

It was during this time in my life that I became aware of the MRS. America contest. Of course, the MISS America pageant was well known across the country, our family rarely missing it on TV each year. It was in 1968 that a friend of mine (Lillian Nordman) entered my name in the Mrs. Iowa contest, and to my amazement, I won! I don't think I'd ever won anything like that in my life before that! I was in shock! That meant I would go on to compete in the national Mrs. America pageant in Minneapolis. I was so excited and nervous to think of it!

I have since read that Burt Nevins, the creator of the original Mrs. America pageant back in 1938, intended it not as a beauty contest, as was the Miss America pageant, but as a celebration of homemaking. During the ten days of the contest, they put us through our paces. We were judged on our ability to prepare a meal, even purchasing the ingredients at the grocery store and then serving it to the judges. We were asked to host an afternoon open house, and arrange flowers for a centerpiece. I'm proud to say that my centerpiece was chosen for a special lunch with Ava Gabor! They even had us set up a tent and cook an outdoor breakfast. Thank goodness husbands were allowed to help, as I couldn't have done it without Don!

First runner up for Mrs. Savings Bond with Burt Nevins and Ava Gabor

We contestants were also asked to show how we would furnish a complete home, picking out everything from flooring to wall paint, and then gluing the paper furnishings into a paper model home. They even interviewed us about money management and required us to take an actual driver's test, both written and driving. There was also a talent component to the contest, so I sang "Danny Boy", accompanying myself on the piano.

IOWA

There was no swimsuit competition, but we were asked to model clothes to show our idea of what a proper married woman should wear. To judge how well we related to children, they asked us to come up with an activity to do with an actual child for fifteen minutes. I read "The Three Bears" book, using finger puppets that I had made. That went well because it was just like teaching school. While the wives were obviously very busy during the ten days of the contest, our husbands had their own special activities including a ten-mile canoe trip down the St. Croix River!

Although I didn't become Mrs. America, I was honored to be runner-up for the title of Mrs. Savings Bond. The entire experience made me feel like such a celebrity! It was the first time I had ever ridden in a convertible in a parade! When Don and I returned home, we were greeted at the airport in Cedar Rapids by a large group of friends, like we were real VIPs! During that year as Mrs. Iowa, I was asked to represent Iowa by giving talks to different groups, riding in several city parades, and being given a key to the city of Mt. Vernon when I visited there.

Mrs. Utah (Joan Fisher from Salt Lake City) was crowned Mrs. America that year, and she and I became friends. On one occasion when she and her husband were visiting Don and I at home in Iowa, she confided that she was sure that the judges were told to pick the winner according to what they thought an ideal American family would look like. She said they were looking for a religious family with three children, including both boys and girls, with a stay-at-home mother who was comfortable speaking to large groups.

In hindsight, I think I have a better perspective on the whole contest. I think that the Mrs. America contest epitomized the American family values of 1950s and 1960s. The "Leave it to Beaver" model of a family with a breadwinner husband, a homemaker wife, children, and a home in the suburbs, was the idealized picture of American families.

As I think of it now, I'm surprised that there were indeed a few contestants that year who were people of color, but society's attitudes at the time were such that they had little chance of winning the title.   I wonder if I myself would have been considered for the contest in later years when I returned to a full-time teaching career. I know I wasn't any less of a mother and wife then, but I wouldn't have fit the mold.

Even with the contest's narrow focus, I think the Mrs. America pageant had value. There's something to be said for providing a way for housewives to be recognized. In some ways, it's remarkable that this conservative view celebrates the work of a housewife, which has been, and so often still is, undervalued in American society.   I think we all like to be recognized for what we do, no matter what it is!

Around that same time, my sister, Joanne's family was also

recognized, winning the All-American Family contest for Ohio. I'd done well as Mrs. Iowa, so another friend urged me to enter our family in the All-American Family contest as well, which we won for Iowa the following year! In 1971, Don and I and the girls headed for Lehigh Acres, Florida, for ten days, as Iowa's All-American Family. Our hometown of Marion played it up big, presenting us with gifts and lots of publicity!

This time, all four of us, Don, Diane, DeLana, and I were busy day and night with the special events. Don even won the golf tournament! Diane and DeLana had fun participating in the children's dance show. For our family talent, we put together a musical group with Diane playing the guitar, DeLana on her flute, and me singing, of course!

The judges seemed to always have their eyes on us, even during meal time, so I told Diane and DeLana they had to use their best manners! The judges also interviewed us often, wanting to know our thoughts on everything! Participating in both contests, Mrs. America and the All-American Family, opened up our Iowa world to attitudes from folks from all over the country. I never dreamed I would have such experiences!

DeLana, 12(holding Tammy), Don, Donna and Diane, 14 getting ready for the All American Family contest in Lehigh Acres, Florida

PART 4

Middle Years
1973 - 1995

"One child, one teacher, one pen, and one book can change the world" -
Malala Yousafzai

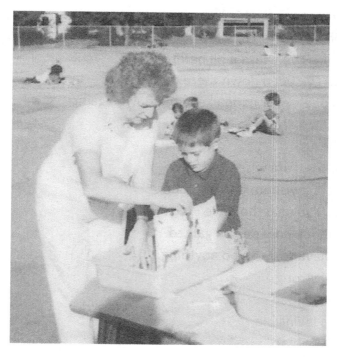

Doing an Eric Carle project outside with a student

Chapter 13
The Times

Equal rights laws made discrimination illegal in the mid-sixties, but it was popular music that helped to change our hearts and attitudes!   It's often our music, not the history books, that best expresses the tempo of society at the time. I think of Helen Reddy's hit song in 1971, "I am Woman", which was a gift for women's rights.

I am woman, hear me roar
In numbers too big to ignore
And I know too much to go back an' pretend.
'Cause I've heard it all before
And I've been down there on the floor
No one's ever gonna keep me down again.

[Chorus]
Oh yes, I am wise
But it's wisdom born of pain.
Yes, I've paid the price
But look how much I gained.
If I have to, I can do anything.
I am strong,
(Strong)
I am invincible,
(Invincible)
I am woman

Then in 1973, the so-called "Battle of the Sexes" took place, televised for the nation to see! It was THE tennis match of the decade between Billie Jean King and Bobby Riggs, and it seemed most everybody was tuned in to watch it. Riggs, who played up his role as a male-chauvinist, actually lost the match, sending a message that women were to be reckoned with!   A shot in the arm for the Women's Movement!

In 1979, I was stunned and heartbroken to learn, that my little sister, Joyce, was splitting up with her husband of ten years. They had married in their last year at the University of Iowa, and after graduation, moved to Connecticut where her husband became a musician in the U.S. Coast Guard Band. All seemed well, with her husband's promising new position, and Joyce's successful teaching career in full swing.

I couldn't help but worry about Joyce, trying to imagine how she would manage to raise their two-year-old daughter on her own, and so far away from family. Divorce was not something I was familiar with, since Joyce was the first person in our extended family to find herself in that situation. In fact, I don't remember ever hearing the word "divorce" when I was child growing up in the 1930s.   Back then, the prevailing thinking was that a woman HAD to have a husband to support her, since divorce so often equaled poverty in America. In fact, any single woman had a difficult time in those days, with so few avenues open to her to support herself.

I suppose Joyce's divorce was a sign of the changing times, as it was becoming more commonplace by the late 70's, and less stigmatized. Women were not so defined as only a wife and mother, and with contraception methods readily available, they had a degree of control over how many children they would have. That fact alone increased their chances of successfully combining a career and a family. Now with more higher paying jobs available to women, they were better able to "go it alone".

Women were entering colleges and universities in ever greater numbers, and with higher education, career opportunities grew rapidly for women. It stands to reason that with more women entering the workplace, work relationships could easily grow into something more. According to Joyce, that had been a factor in her divorce as the Coast Guard Band had begun admitting women to their all-male ranks.

Although I didn't feel bold enough to ever participate in the women's marches of the era, maybe because I was "an old married lady with children", I know now that I was the beneficiary with ever growing career opportunities coming my way. Doors began to open for me, as I became the teacher that others came to for advice, not the other way around. I took a leadership role in mentoring many student teachers through these years as well, and, in the 1980s, was one of four teachers in our school district to be chosen to become a "Math Their Way" instructor to teachers all over the country, including Hawaii! I ended up teaching fifty-one workshops in twenty-one years. I felt as if I'd grown wings!

With my expanding teaching career, I barely noticed that there was inequality all around me in the schools. Most all the elementary school teachers were women, while all the senior administrative staff, including principals and superintendents (those getting the highest salaries) were men. Even the Board of Education was predominantly made up of men in Cedar Rapids. I didn't think much about it at the time. That's just the way it was. For the most part, women had to be patient in obtaining positions of power and authority, not only in education, but in other arenas as well.

My life felt settled during this time, with both Don and I now middle-aged, established in our teaching careers, and more financially secure. We felt like a dream had come true in 1972, when we came back to our rural roots, moving to a home in the country that even included a small acreage. But what we saw on the nightly news presented a very different backdrop to our life, one of struggle for so many Americans at that time. Activism for equal rights, not just for women, but for black and gay people, continued to intensify.

My sense was that many white Americans, who were the vast majority of the population in Iowa, didn't know quite what to make of what was going on in the country, but movies of the day provided a window of understanding. As early as 1967, Sidney Portier's portrayal of an educated, well-spoken black man paved the way. I remember well "Guess Who's Coming to Dinner" bringing a liberal thinking white couple face to face with the unthinkable notion of their daughter falling in love with a black man. Keep in mind that interracial marriage was still illegal in seventeen states (not Iowa!) up until six months before the movie appeared in theaters.

Shortly after that, came another of Portier's movies, "In the Heat of the Night", about a black police investigator from Philadelphia who came to visit his mother in the South and found himself in the midst of racist practices and attitudes. That was, until the town's sheriff began to realize that he needed this "nigger's" help to solve a murder case. At the time, my personal interactions with people of color were still infrequent, perhaps because it was Marion, small-town white Iowa, not New York City or Chicago. Notably in 1971, I began working with a black woman (Barb Osgood), a new teacher in our district whom I was assigned to mentor. She was a joy for me to work with, and we remain friends today. I learned firsthand that our similarities far outweighed our difference in skin color!

Popular TV shows also helped us sort out their thinking and even laugh at ourselves, with shows like "All in the Family" pitting the conservative father, Archie Bunker, against his liberal thinking son-in-law, "Meathead", in a lovable and hilarious way. Then there was "Sanford and Son", a comedy that give insight into the life and thinking of a hard-working, traditional black man and his forward-thinking son. "The Brady Bunch" showed Americans that a blended family with two previously divorced parents was "OK". "Mary Tyler Moore" portrayed the life of a young woman who was able to make a career in the "man's world" of a newsroom. As I think about it now, I can see that the writers of these shows knew that comedy had the greatest impact!

It's not surprising to me that people are tribal by nature, preferring folks that look like them, act like them, and think like them. I don't think there's anything inherently wrong with that, except when it prevents us from seeing similarities that link us in other ways to different folks. In my lifetime, I've seen situations where we can't seem to see past a person who looks or acts "different".

Teaching young children all my life, it became my goal to instill in them a way to find connection, or at the very least, an understanding of another child whom they might initially consider an outsider. I believe that teaching children is much more than providing them with skills in "reading, writing, and 'rithmetic". It's as much about encouraging youngsters to grow into well-adjusted, caring adults who have a positive impact on sustaining a loving society. I feel that's why teaching has been so rewarding for me, knowing that I was leaving the world a better place than I found it. That is the joy of teaching!

On May Day each year, my class told the history of May Day and did the Maypole Dance around the Maypole.

Chapter 14
Back to My Country Roots

You know what they say, "you can take the girl out of the country, but you can't take the country out of the girl"! So true for me! Both Don and I had grown up on a farm, and realized our dream of rural living in 1972 when we moved to a home in the country! Unlike our house in town, this one had been built about twenty years prior, and I think now that I must have seen a newspaper story about it back when it was first built, and thought to myself, wouldn't that be just the place for us?! Of course, I never thought it could ever be!

We weren't looking for elegance in a new home, but we longed for the space to do all the things we loved. Our new place had six-and-a-half acres of land, so we were able to more than double the size of our garden, adding flower beds everywhere I found a spot, doing much of our own landscaping. Don discovered the zen of mowing, spending hours on his new riding lawn mower. The acreage had a small barn that was just right for a few horses, and it even had a pretty little creek running through the property.

Unfortunately, the creek overflowed into our back yard every spring, though the water never came up to the house, thankfully!

Looking out the back window toward the horse barn and creek

The house was a sprawling ranch, all on one level, white with a brick base and black shutters. I was taken by its spacious rooms, with storage abounding everywhere I looked! There were plenty of bedrooms for family visits, and with Mom and Dad getting older, our home soon became the hub for family gatherings including those special times when my sister Joanne's family came from Ohio. Don and I enjoyed our new role, hosting all our family holiday dinners around our huge dining room table. Wonderful times!

The house had a full basement, the entire footprint of the upstairs, so we had plenty of room for our old-fashioned upright piano, a ping pong table, and even a pool table. I was thrilled to finally have some things I'd always wished for, like a huge tub for soaking clothes, a gigantic work table for crafting, plantings, and for canning and freezing vegetables from our garden, as well as a separate area for my sewing machine. The basement was a pleasant place to spend time since it was airy and bright, built at ground level on the back side, opening into the back yard with a picture window and a lovely patio for cookouts.

I don't usually think of my houseplants as something noteworthy, but the fern that grew in our new living room was amazing! It was just a bitty little plant when I bought it, but that room was the perfect spot for it, getting the morning light from the (nearly) floor-to-ceiling windows. It seemed to explode, quickly becoming too large to fit on the coffee table so mom gave me a plant stand for it. It eventually got so big that I had to sell it, but I couldn't resist starting over with another little fern. But in time, it too was almost as wide as it was tall, nearly four feet across!

Don and I quickly got to know and enjoy our new neighbors, though there were only a few on our country road. Right next door to us were *Carolyn and Mel Holubar(below)*, and we

seemed to be always borrowing things from each other, like a cup of sugar or a tool. Keep in mind that driving into town was only a few miles, but of course, we didn't just drive to the store for one item!

Me with our neighbors (and fellow Kiwanians!) Carolyn and Mel Holubar. Barb Feller-who was Marion's historical Granger House director (center) and Emil Kovac Kiwanis friend(right)

Neighbors Nancy Kratzer, Martha White and Jo Bouslog on our porch

On the other side of us lived Martha and Winfield White, lovely neighbors also, but with an inconvenient little ditch between our houses. Don soon set about to do something about that! Coincidentally at that time, the town of Marion was replacing sidewalks, so for many weeks, Don and I quickly changed into work clothes after school and drove into Marion with our trailer to gather broken pieces of the old sidewalks to fill in our ditch. The property owners were only too happy to have us remove the huge slabs of broken concrete. I remember that it took both of us to lift many pieces into our trailer! But in the end, we were successful in filling in the ditch, as we finished the job by adding dirt dug up from another neighbor's yard when they put in an in-ground swimming pool right at that time!

The girls were older now, as DeLana headed to junior high, and Diane now a sophomore in high school, both riding a school bus for the first time! Suddenly they were the "new kids on the block" at their new schools. DeLana recalls how the bus experience, in particular, was a big change for her, noticing that kids from the country had a looser interpretation of proper behavior on the bus than the quieter city kids who came onto the bus as it neared the school. Not that the "country kids" were bad or mean, but they were much more relaxed in following the rules. DeLana says it took a while for her to figure out quite where she fit in!

Diane recalls her most surprising memory when we first moved to the country was the amazing sound of all the birds, especially as she walked down the lane to catch the school bus, past the huge walnut tree in the front yard. It always made her think of the Hitchcock movie "The Birds", as they were so loud, although not menacing like the movie!

Steve always wanted ducks. DeLana got him four ducks for his first Father's day but the neighbor's hunting dog got into the cage and made it a short-lived venture. Our dogs, Tammy and Tesha were very interested too.

Of course, we brought our two dear little Toy Manchester terrier dogs, Tammy and Tesha, with us from our house in town, "rats" as my dad used to refer to them! Although we didn't have livestock like a working farm, Diane and DeLana both chipped in $100 to buy a horse that they named Sugar. We knew she was pregnant at the time we bought her, but we were all shocked to look out the window that next morning to see that we suddenly had two! The girls named the colt Bullet because of a black spot on his forehead.

When DeLana was in high school, she had her horse, Brandy, bred to a registered male. DeLana named her colt R-Rox, and dedicated herself to breaking the colt herself, with some help and advice from a horse trainer. Don even built a training ring for her! Quite something to see Rox following DeLana's leg signals to know what gait DeLana commanded!

Our house in the country now became the natural gathering place whenever Hoptons visited from Ohio, with Mom and

Dad driving up to stay with us as well. Always a houseful! My sister, Joanne's three children (Pam, Greg, and Terri) were around the same age as Diane and DeLana, and what fun the cousins had together at our place in the country! The cousins maintained their closeness even though they only got to see each other a few times a year.

The cousins even formed their own club with a hand-sewn flag to represent it! They continued the tradition of planning and performing shows for us parents, with Pam (the oldest cousin) taking over my sister Joyce's role as director, who was now living in Connecticut. Near the end of each visit, they presented their new show, charging us adults a few pennies admission!

I clearly remember the fun times the cousins had sliding down the bank alongside our creek, turning into muddy, mucky messes! One afternoon when I was watching them having fun on the bank, I told them to wait while I got my camera to catch the moment. When I returned, they all had covered their bodies, from head to toe, with the black mud. What a sight they were, and what fun they had! Fortunately, we had a shower and laundry room just inside the basement door, so the clean-up was simple, and even the adults had a good laugh!

In 1970, Joanne and Rick surprised us by adding another cousin with their baby son, Brad, and four years later, baby Brian, making a twenty-year spread between their oldest child, Pam, and their youngest. We all adored the new baby cousins! A few years after Brian's birth, yet another cousin was added when my younger sister, Joyce, had her daughter, Carolyn, in 1977. Carolyn was more like a little sister than a cousin to Diane and DeLana, who were in college by then!

I didn't like to think of my little girls leaving home, but I was so proud to see both of them turning into capable and caring young women.

Diane graduated from Linn Mar High School in 1975, and, like me when I was a teen, she was a regular babysitter for several families, even spending a summer as a nanny for the Staley family's three girls. She (again like me) was active in school activities, especially singing groups.

In the summer of 1977, between semesters at the University of Iowa, Diane showed her adventurous side when she flew out to Connecticut to stay with my sister, Joyce, for a week, to help after the birth of Joyce's daughter, Carolyn. This had to give Diane pause since she'd never flown in an airplane before, certainly not by herself! Joyce's husband was away on tour with the Coast Guard Band then, so Joyce would have had to manage by herself with a new baby.

Traditionally, mothers often stayed to help their daughters after the birth of a child, and I know Mom would have wanted to be there, but she was getting into her seventies. I thought of going myself, but was busier than ever presenting writing workshops every summer to teachers around the school district. Joyce recalls how grateful she was for Diane to be there with her as a brand-new mom! I believe to this day, that this special time Diane spent with Joyce and baby Carolyn cemented the bond between them.

Diane majored in elementary education at the university, with a specialty in reading instruction, eventually receiving her Master's degree in developmental reading. I think back to the times when I scolded Diane as a child for always having her nose in a book! Again, her adventurous spirit led her to do part of her student teaching at an elementary school in Exeter, England, living with a family there and getting to know the culture as well as the schools. She recalls that everyone there wanted to call her "Di" since Lady Diana Spencer was becoming the sweetheart of England.

Diane's teaching career began as a Reading Specialist in the Fox Valley School District in the tiny town of Cantril, Iowa, soon organizing both the church and city libraries and leading the church youth group, as well as teaching. After five years in Cantril, Diane took a job in Manchester, Iowa, closer to home, where she found her "teaching home" until her eventual retirement.

DeLana and Diane were similar in some ways, rarely causing Don and I concern throughout their childhood and teen years, but so different in other ways. As a teenager, DeLana was more "into" her horse, spending long hours training Rox. Also, DeLana always seemed to approach things from an artistic perspective. She created a private quiet space in her bedroom, removing the doors from one of her closets, with

 her friend's autographs spread across the closet wall, and then hanging pink shimmery beads as a sort of curtain in front. In fact, her whole room screamed PINK!

I remember the little notes that DeLana often left for Don and me to read when we returned home from teaching, like "There's a surprise in the fridge". DeLana loved to cook and many nights would have supper ready for us! Like Diane, she was active in high school, with singing groups and playing flute in the band. She was selected to be in the very first Linn Mar Marching Band Flag Corps. We moms got together with the girls to design and sew their outfits and their red and white flags. They did look sharp with their white boots!

 DeLana took all the art classes they offered in high school, and went on to graduate from Mount Mercy College in just three years, right here in Cedar Rapids, with a degree in art education. Always looking to economize, Delana lived at home during college and continued her high school job, working thirty hours a week at our local HyVee grocery store while carrying a full load of college classes!

Little did we know that DeLana's job at HyVee would be life-changing, since that is where DeLana met Steve Hubler, whom she dated until they married after college. Steve became like the son we never had, so thoughtful and kind, often helping us with our huge yard and gardens.

When DeLana and Steve got engaged in 1980, I thought of Mom's words to me growing up, warning that we girls should never marry a boy from a Catholic family since our children would have to grow up in the Catholic faith. But I could see that DeLana and Steve cared deeply for each other, and Mom's words from long ago no longer rang true for me.

It was such fun to plan their wedding with DeLana! They were married at the historic Marion First Presbyterian Church on May 23, 1981. The bridesmaids, including Diane as maid of honor, were all in pink, or I should say, in mauve, as our artist daughter explained. Two of Steve's brothers and a friend served as groomsmen. The church was full with family and friends. Of course, Hoptons from Ohio were all there, as well as Mom and Dad. Joyce flew in from Connecticut to sing "Longer Than" by Dan Fogelberg, which DeLana and Steve had chosen.

Joyce's little daughter, Carolyn, was the flower girl. She was only three years old at the time, and Joyce admits now that she should have used better judgment in expecting

Carolyn to be at ease walking down the aisle into a room full of strangers. In retrospect, it would have helped Carolyn if her mom had not been sitting up front, apart from the pews where Carolyn would be. In any case, when Carolyn saw her mom up front in the sanctuary, she burst into tears, calling out "Mommy". Cousin Terri Hopton quickly escorted her outside and the ceremony continued on beautifully. Carolyn was all smiles afterward when she was reunited with her mom!

I felt a little sad that Don and I were about to begin a new chapter of our lives as "empty nesters", but we were glad that both Diane and DeLana lived nearby. And, best of all, we were soon to discover the joys of becoming grandparents!

From left: Jeff Hubler, Jean Spearman, John Hubler, DeLana, Steve,
Diane Bean, Teresa Shaffer, Kevin Horman
In Front: Carolyn Werden and Jamie Hubler

DeLana and Steve with their "baby Tiffani"

Chapter 15
Just the Two of Us

I was of two minds, when both Diane and DeLana left our family "nest", sad to think that my active parenting days were behind me, but so proud and happy that both our girls had successfully prepared themselves for their teaching careers and were making their way in the world, out on their own. When you're raising children, your life tends to revolve around their needs and activities, but during these years, Don and I began to increasingly focus once again on our own interests, although we looked forward to making time for our anticipated grandchildren!

My emotions were running high at Dad's funeral in 1983, having recently found out that DeLana was expecting their first child, our first grandchild and my parents' first great-grandchild. The juxtaposition of Dad lying in the open casket in front of me and a pregnant DeLana sitting in a pew behind me, made it clear that life is a circle. My dad's life had ended, but a new life was beginning, and I had to adjust to that cycle.

Dad was eighty-one when he died, and had been having health issues for a while. It began with trouble swallowing because of swollen glands that was eventually diagnosed as lymphoma. Chemotherapy sent it into remission, but within the next year, he was experiencing difficulty with shortness of breath that made it difficult for him to do anything physical, even walking down the lane to the mailbox. Again, he underwent chemotherapy at the University Hospital, this time for emphysema. He had never smoked a day in his life, but it was thought that all his years of breathing in grain dust on the farm had damaged his lungs.

 Mom was only seventy-five when she died six months after Dad's passing. Her declining health had gone undiagnosed for over a year by a family doctor she had been seeing in nearby Nichols, Iowa, complaining to him about pain and a lump in her abdomen. As it happened, I had stopped by on one of my regular visits to the farm one day, to find Mom looking pale and having lost so much weight! I immediately got her in that very day to see doctors at Mercy Hospital in Iowa City who diagnosed her with advanced colon cancer that the doctors there said could have been removed if it had been caught earlier.

I know that both my parents could have had longer and healthier lives if they'd understood more about the importance of good nutrition, exercise, and getting excellent medical attention right away. Although they would have had some health insurance with the passage of Medicare in 1965, their mindset was such that they didn't go to a doctor until they were at death's door!

Don and I were soon to take over my parent's role as grandparents. DeLana and Steve's daughters, Ashley, Megan, and Samantha, were born just two years apart from each other. We quickly discovered the joys of grandparenting, so happy to have little ones in our lives once again! Their house was only about fifteen minutes from ours, so we were fortunate to be able to share many fun times with them as they were growing up.

How they loved our place in the country! They would jump out of the family car and run around our yard picking an apple or a pear from one of our fruit trees, or grabbing a fresh carrot or a pea pod from one of our gardens. And when strawberries were in season, they would pop one in their mouth or grab a bunch of grapes from our vines. Don put up a high swing from the huge walnut tree in our front yard that made the girls squeal with delight every time!

Like the cousins before them, the girls slid down our muddy creek bank, and sometimes even caught one of the tiny fish or frogs to throw back in the water. Sometimes we just sat quietly on the bank and listened to the water ripple over the rocks. In winter, they flew down our sloped back yard on their sleds, or played "Old Maid" inside. I don't know if they ever knew that Grandpa (Don) had clipped a tip off the Old Maid card, so he always knew where it was!

Donna, Megan,5, Don, Samantha, 3, and Ashley,7 in 1991

Of course, reading books to them was my greatest joy, and we always got creative with the stories, as I made a breakfast of "green eggs and ham" after we read Dr. Seuss's book. They dug for treasure (pennies) in the sand after we read pirate stories. The girls created their own special place in a large cupboard off our kitchen, that just fit three small chairs, with a little step for writing or drawing. They wrote out a sign for it, "Our Undergrond [Underground] World", that I still have to this day to show the grandchildren's children, my eight great-grandchildren!

So much seemed to be happening at about the same time: the deaths of my parents, the births of my granddaughters, and now a new teaching position at a different school after thirteen years at Hiawatha School in Cedar Rapids. I was reluctant to leave the staff at Hiawatha, such a helpful and fun group, but the principal and I didn't see eye-to-eye, and I couldn't pass up the chance to work for Jack Christiansen, the new principal at Arthur School. His first interview question to me was to describe my classroom. My immediate response was "organized chaos", explaining that my students know

where learning materials are and how to use them, but that the level of activity in the room may look chaotic.

Geri Hasley-One of the dearest enduring friends that I made while I was teaching at Arthur.

Kathy Conley was the best principal that I ever had- with Jo Bader, Sweet Adeline and teaching friend and Samantha

Singing at Carnegie Hall with me, Linda Mallard and Bonnie Spear

More singing opportunities opened up for me in 1976, when one of our neighbors, Shari Staley, who knew of my love for singing, asked me to join the local Sweet Adeline's barbershop chorus. It was called the Cedar Rhapsody Chorus, eventually changing the name to the Cedar Sounds Chorus. It turned out to be just the right thing for me to be singing with a group of women that soon felt like "family"!

Our performances were so much fun, singing for many community events, dressed in our identical shimmery dresses! My sewing skills came in handy once again, sewing all my Sweet Adelines outfits, even organizing an assembly line of other members at my house to get dresses made for others. But I hated the heavy makeup required for us at performances, especially the false eyelashes!

Cedar Rhapsody Sweet Adelines winning3rd at International in London. I'm the starred one.

The chorus was at its height then, even winning third place at the Sweet Adelines International Competition in London at the royal Albert Hall, as well as performing all over the city! After London, our chorus was invited to sing at Carnegie Hall in NYC, and such a thrill it was! My sister, Joyce, and daughter, Carolyn, attended from their home in Connecticut, about a three-hour train ride. Diane flew out from Iowa to join them in taking the train into New York for the performance. I felt so happy to be performing for family there!

In order to defray the cost of our trips, we joined in many fundraising efforts, like painting a member's mobile home, selling food at every University of Iowa Hawkeye football game for over 20 years, making crafts to sell at bazaars, and operating a food stand at the Cedar Rapids Ice Arena for hockey games. Probably our most unusual (and our most challenging) fundraiser was working for Amana Winery, in their fields picking dandelions and clover for them to make wine. It always seemed to be on days when it was a hundred degrees, with bugs and bees swarming all around us! Working together like that really bonded our group!

My longtime Sweet Adeline director, Sally Eggleston. She was an amazing director and an international judge for SA.

I had a long history of throat problems that still plagued me during this time. I had not been able to sing for almost a year prior to our Carnegie Hall appearance while I underwent throat therapy. But through Sweet Adeline's, I learned strategies to help me avoid stressing my vocal cords. I also became more confident with my singing when our director, Sally Eggleston, asked if I would consider singing in the baritone harmony section, not the lead melody that I was used to. I didn't think I could do that, but Sally encouraged me to try it. That was one more instance when someone else's belief in me enabled me to stretch myself to succeed at something new!

Don-1950

Don-1985

The Army Reserves were a big part of Don's life for much of our marriage. In 1974, he was invited to be the West Point Liaison Officer for our section of Iowa. That meant he spent two weeks every fall and spring talking to high school students about becoming a cadet at West Point. Don was so successful that they went from NO recruits before he started, to reaching their full quota within one year! Soon West Point scheduled him to train cadets there every summer.

We turned it into a family trip one year, but at that time, women were not allowed on base, not as cadets, nor even to visit. While we were there, I had to spend the whole day at our nearby motel by myself, while Diane and DeLana were allowed to spend the day with Don, touring West Point and even eating with the cadets. We women still had work to do to gain equal rights back then, although I believe that it was just a year or two later that women were finally admitted to be West Point cadets.

Don taught gym classes at Wright Elementary School for most of his teaching career, but in addition to his regular teaching, in later years, he was asked to be one of the girls' basketball coaches at Washington High School, also in Cedar Rapids. So successful were his teams, that they won their tournaments almost every year!

Don never strayed from his beloved golf. He played in two leagues, traveling all over Iowa with the Cancer Golf Card, which raised money for cancer research. (in his retirement years, he was a golf ranger for the Amana and

Twin Pines Golf Courses). It was during this time, that Don also began taking annual fishing trips with "the guys" to Canada.

My teaching career was also expanding in new directions. In 1985, I was sent by the district, along with three other teachers, to attend a week-long Math Their Way workshop, for grades Kindergarten through second grade. It was a very "hands-on" approach that fit my style of teaching, using manipulatives more than workbooks. We four teachers were expected to pilot the new program in our classrooms in the fall, and to begin the process of introducing it to other teachers in the huge Cedar Rapids district, eventually branching out to teach summer workshops to teachers all over the United States!

Traveling around the country to be a "teacher of teachers" was one of the most rewarding and challenging experiences in my life, continuing even after retirement from full time teaching. But I have to admit that it was a high energy proposition for me, as I had to prepare and pack up boxloads of math materials, and then once at the workshop location, I had to get materials organized and ready for the teachers who would be attending.

On the coast in Oahu with Don and Diane

I found myself in far flung parts of the country, from Hawaii to Boston, sometimes flying out, but if it was closer to home, I drove, and sometimes Don and Diane would join me in the adventure of experiencing a new place. Keep in mind that this was a time long before GPS was available, but somehow, I always managed to find my destinations, even in driving rain!

Don retired from teaching in 1986, filling in his time with substitute teaching, sometimes as a substitute for our daughter, Diane, as a reading teacher, but he soon began a tradition of golfing in Biloxi, Mississippi, for sometimes as long as six weeks.   He made new friends there, and even encouraged some of his Iowa golfing buddies to join him there.

Travel was a passion that Don and I shared our entire married life, including so many football trips over the years like the Rose Bowl in Pasadena, the 'Gator Bowl in Orlando, the Peach Bowl in Atlanta, and the Holiday Bowl in San Diego. While we had visited so many places around the country, it wasn't until 1984 when we ventured outside the U.S. for a European vacation. An eye-opening

experience! In later years, when our grandchildren were old enough, we began a tradition of taking an extended family vacation with everyone, starting with Disneyworld in 1994!

In August, 1993, Don and I decided to sell our beloved country home. We were getting older, and, as you can imagine, it was just too much for us take care of on our own. The year that we moved was the same year that Cedar Rapids was experiencing the highest floods we had had! Flood water seeped into so many basements, including ours which had never flooded before. What a mess!

The timing of the move to a smaller house in town (what we thought would be our retirement home) turned out to be when Carolyn, Joyce's daughter, who was then in middle school, had planned to visit us by herself. What a life-saver she was in helping us get everything packed up! A trip she'd probably prefer to forget, although she never complained the whole time!

The last thing we moved from our country home was everything from our garage and little outbuilding, so we loaded our old pickup with barbed wire, boards, and other junk. The pickup sat in the driveway of our new home for almost two weeks, while we waited for the yard to have its final grading done.

We imagined that our new neighbors probably thought they had the "Beverly Hillbillies" moving into their neighborhood! But they didn't seem to hold it against us, as we soon became active in the neighborhood parties. On one of those occasions, Don and I even dressed up as Jed and Granny Clampett from the Beverly Hillbillies! I still have the gray wig I wore for the part of Granny!

PART 5

Retirement Years

1995 to the Present

"Carve your name on hearts, not tombstones. A legacy is etched into the minds of others and the stories they share about you." –

Shannon L. Alder

At Hole 5 on Gardner Golf Course in Marion, IA

Chapter 16
The Times

There was a riddle, sort of a joke, that started going around in the '80s that stumped so many people at the time. It went something like this: "A father and son were in a car accident where the father was killed. The ambulance brought the son to the hospital. He needed immediate surgery. In the operating room, a doctor came in and looked at the little boy and said I can't operate on him. He is my son. How can that be?" For today's young folks, the answer seems simple, the surgeon was his mother, but back then, doctors were men and women were nurses for the most part, so we were all stumped. Who would have a picture in their mind that it was a female surgeon?!

Stereotypes about the role of women were gradually fading in other areas as well. Just the other day, I read that Barbara Walters, the well-known female TV news pioneer, had died. Barbara Walters had been a fixture in the world of reporting most of my adult life, and I never thought much about it. But the newspaper article was quite lengthy, outlining her accomplishments, noting that Barbara Walters was the first woman to become a TV news anchor. Turn on any news channel today to see female newscasters everywhere!

When I retired in 1995, I was not the first to step outside the boundaries of homemaker, but I was not in the majority when I successfully combined a career with married life. That was uncommon for married women when I was growing up, from the days when the stay-at-home mom was the norm, and wives were expected to cook and clean for their breadwinning husbands.

I never thought of myself as revolutionary, but I was living proof that a woman could have a professional life while raising a family, something my mother, with all of her gifts, could only dream about, although she had had the wisdom to encourage me to do just that. DeLana recalls that when she was growing up, she was always proud that I had a career while many of her friends' mothers did not.

Women in abusive relationships still had a difficult time. It wasn't until 1994, when President Clinton signed into law the Violence Against Women Act, providing funding to help victims of domestic violence. Women now had more options if they found themselves in that situation. Even one of my extended family members was affected when she was able to leave an abusive marriage because her career opportunities enabled her to support herself comfortably on her own.

Women were making news every day, even in politics, which, like so many arenas, had previously been a man's domain. In the late nineties, Madeleine Albright became the first female Secretary of State. Hillary Clinton became the first female candidate for President, and in 2021, Kamala Harris was elected the first woman to become Vice President.

Blacks too were making strides in achieving equal opportunities, most notably, Barack Obama, who in 2009, became our first African American President. I'm sure I wasn't the only person that thought that could never happen! I had so much admiration for him as our President, but it was clear in the aftermath, that there was a segment of American society that was not ready for a non-white President.

Civil rights for gay Americans were also gaining momentum, although in my mind, they lagged behind women and people of color. By this time, homosexuality was no longer illegal in the U.S., but crimes of hate could be deadly for anyone who was openly gay. In 1998, Matthew Shepard, a twenty-one-year-old student at the University of Wyoming, was attacked and left to die because he was gay.

It wasn't until 2010 that President Obama signed the repeal of "Don't Ask Don't "Tell" rule, enabling gay and lesbian people to serve OPENLY in the military. The Supreme Court voted 5-4 that year that same-sex couples' right to marry is guaranteed. I'm proud to say that Iowa was one of the states that led the way in issuing marriage licenses to same-sex couples, adding that they may also adopt children, and further, banning discrimination based on sexual orientation in employment, housing, and public accommodations. Again, our family was touched by this decision, when one of my granddaughters was able to marry her female partner, and now have two precious daughters.

Saying goodbye on my last day of teaching-with Anne Berneir, Miranda Fuchs, and Paula Clymer

1995 was not only the year I retired, but also the year that cell phones came into common usage, and in my opinion, revolutionized our lives. I must interject here that if you are a young person reading this, and born during this time, it may feel redundant to read the rest of this chapter, as all these changes are a "given". But understand that for those of us in our senior years, it has been a time of remarkable change.

166

To think that a young girl from a farm in the 1930s talked on a party line through a big rectangular wooden phone box on the wall, and now, I can even see the faces of the folks I'm speaking to when I use Facetime on my cell phone. Suddenly, a phone was not used solely for conversation, but more like a mini-computer. My cell phone travels everywhere with me, so that I can talk to anyone from wherever I am, to as far away as I want without feeling that I have to keep the conversation short to avoid those long-distance fees of long ago.

I can take photos and even videos anytime on my cell phone, check messages on my email, and see what my friends are up to on Facebook! It gives me the latest weather, has a little flashlight, a compass, a calculator, etc. The list is endless! It was the Internet that enabled computers and I-phones to replace books as our primary source of information.

When Diane and DeLana were small, I remember that Don sold World Books, sets of encyclopedias, to supplement his teaching salary. Parents asked for his help because they trusted him! These books were a staple of many American households back then, full of what-we-thought-at-the-time was all the information about everything we needed to know. I wonder if libraries even have encyclopedias today?! Actually, the term library is somewhat outdated now, as they are more accurately called media centers, to include computers and all electronic information sources.

In today's world, we can not only find historical facts and medical information on the Internet, but we can also locate nearby restaurants, even making a reservation right from our phone or computer. I can place an online order with any company at any time. I almost forgot to mention the all-important GPS function on my cell phone that would have been a godsend when I was finding my way traveling the country with my Math Their Way workshops!

Of course, there have been so many other improvements in technology, such as televisions. When I was in my teen years, we got our first TV, with a tiny black-and-white picture, having just three channels that were often so snowy you had to strain to see the picture, and needing constant adjustment to keep the picture from scrolling. As we are accustomed to today, TVs are huge, often hanging on the wall, with a seemingly limitless number of channels with a crystal clear picture, offering streaming options so you can watch shows and movies at any time, as often as you like, even on your phone.

It goes without saying that advances in technology have transformed our kitchens. As a child, we had a huge stove that we "fed" wood, and later coal. I remember that a few years later, we were fortunate to "upgrade" to one of the kerosene fueled stoves. I can't forget our ice box that was exactly that, a box that held a block of ice to keep things cold, with regular deliveries from the ice man. My "ice box" today is a spacious side-by-side refrigerator/freezer, which we all take for granted. And try getting along without your microwave for a day!

Refrigeration also made possible air-conditioners, first in stores, theaters, hotels, and then in homes. We take for granted that our cars will be warm in winter and cool in summer, no longer suffering with the temperature. When I was young, car heaters were rudimentary, and air-conditioning wasn't even thought of in cars, only added in later years as a luxury option if you could afford to pay for it. Of course, self-driving cars are on the horizon right now. What next?!

Medical technology was also keeping pace, and Don and I were fortunate to be living at a time when so many advanced medical procedures were available. We had a history of good health for most of our adult lives, rarely missing a day of work, but with our advancing years, doctors' appointments were increasing. Our first big scare came in 1996, when Don needed to have quadruple heart bypass surgery, not a common procedure at the time.

A few years later in 1999, Don had one of his knees replaced, and over the next twenty-five years, had his other knee replaced, as well as a redo of the first knee replacement, something unheard of for my parent's generation. Don said that the techniques used in each of his subsequent knee surgeries was easier and so much improved.

In 2007, Don went for expert care at the Mayo Clinic in Rochester, Minnesota, for back surgery to put several plates in his spine. As you can imagine, this was a major undertaking for us. It took over three hours for us to drive there, requiring Diane and me to stay at a nearby motel for six days until Don was able to travel home, followed by a lengthy period of physical therapy and healing. But in the end, it was a successful operation, although he had shots for back pain throughout the rest of his life.

I also had increasing health concerns. From 1999 until 2018, I had kidney stones every two years, but the first time was the scariest! I couldn't imagine what was happening. I thought I was having appendicitis! I was substitute teaching that day, and began having excruciating pain on my side! Thankfully, it was almost dismissal time, and I asked one of my little boys to tell the office that I needed help. DeLana was able to come to

169

rush me to the hospital, but by the time she got there, I was vomiting in the nurse's room at school!

As it turned out, a kidney stone was causing all the pain. Now kidney stone removal was nothing new, as such operations dated back to the Middle Ages (though sometimes fatal), but I didn't like the idea of surgery. I ended up spending two nights at the hospital with pain pills, lots of walking, and drinking water until it felt like it was coming out of my ears! But ultimately, those modern-day techniques helped me pass the stone without needing surgery.

In the ensuing years, I also had had several surgeries, one for cardiac ablation, cataract surgery, two stents put in my heart for a blockage, as well as having a blood clot in the left artery in my neck dissolved. But it wasn't until 2020, when the country and the world were thrown into the unknown by the deadly Covid pandemic that swept through our lives. Hospitals were soon overflowing, and so many folks were dying!

Medical advances had all but wiped out small pox, scarlet fever, polio, whooping cough, even measles and chicken pox, in the developing world, so it was a jolt for American society to suddenly live in fear of leaving their homes. Overnight, we were isolated, hunkering down at home, only going out for necessities, avoiding groups of people. Masks were the rule of the day if you had to go out, and to stay six feet apart from everyone else. Drug companies were scrambling to find a vaccine.

Businesses were struggling with so few customers, and restaurants were organizing ways to provide outdoor seating which was less contagious. Movie theaters and entertainment venues were going out of business, and even Broadway came to a halt. Schools went virtual for the first time. If they could, many people worked from their computers at home to avoid human contact. Covid variants still keep popping up, though the effects are lessened through vaccinations and boosters.

On May 5, 2022, I did get Covid, even with all my precautions, but I didn't get very sick, probably because my shots were all up to date. I did have to isolate completely from everyone, even family, for the requisite ten days. I cannot help but wonder if we'll ever be completely free from the threat of Covid. There's talk now of needing a yearly Covid shot, just as we do for the flu. My sense is that society has not fully recovered from the isolation of Covid, although there are signs that we're starting to return to a state of more normalcy.

And so it was that, almost imperceptibly, our everyday vocabulary began in incorporate new words like Wi-Fi, app, spam, scam, hacked, social media, Google search, texting, virtual learning, zoom meetings, etc. I feel lucky to have been the beneficiary of not only modern medical miracles, but also of the myriad of the other technological advances of the time!

Maybe the portrayal of American life in the Jetson's animated TV sitcom from the 1960s was not as far off the mark as we thought at the time! We seem primed to go from self-driving to flying cars! As futurist Ray Kurzweil explains it, change is happening exponentially, that is to say, "if I take 30 steps linearly, I get to 30. If I take 30 steps exponentially, I get a million"! I can't imagine what the next one hundred years will look like!

Chapter 17
My Life's Partner

On June 19, 2017, my life changed in an instant when Don suddenly died. He had been my life's partner through our sixty-two years of marriage. I suppose it was not a total surprise, because in the weeks prior, he had given me a few scares by passing out for about five minutes on three different days. I called an ambulance each time, and each time,

everything was normal by the time they got him to the hospital. The doctors decided to send him for further testing and rehabilitation to the Hiawatha Care Center here in town, but they again found nothing, and he was home after only two weeks. I breathed a sigh of relief.

Clockwise from top: Steve, Brock, Greg, Joben, and Don on Father's Day 2017(the day before he died)

About a month later, while my niece, Carolyn and her family were visiting from Connecticut, Don was in good spirits, good-naturedly kidding around with our eight-year-old great-nephew, Brian, as he so often liked to have fun with the little kids. Little did we know that those were to be his last words. Shortly afterwards, he went out to his car where I found him leaned back in the seat unconscious. I again rode with him in the ambulance to the hospital, where Diane, DeLana, Steve, and Samantha met us. We all stayed with Don until he died, although he never woke.

Mackenzie, Carolyn and Jordyn Mershon with Brian in front

With a houseful of company and funeral arrangements to be made, you can imagine that I had little chance to even acknowledge my grief. I was so grateful to have Diane, DeLana, and DeLana's husband, Steve, at my side every step of the way with the incredible amount of paperwork, phone calls, and legwork that faced me in "undoing" Don's many life connections. As my sister, Joanne, had alerted me after her husband's sudden death some years before, there is much to attend to in closing out a life.

I was thankful in that moment, that years prior, after both our parents died, Don and I had begun making funeral arrangements for ourselves. We had gone together to the funeral home to arrange for our services and even paid for everything then. We wrote an outline of the program, including the music we wanted. We had previously purchased our burial plots, so all those decisions were made. But even with that done, my daughters and I spent hours canceling Don's bank accounts, credit cards, subscriptions, memberships, etc.

Don's service was held at Murdock's Funeral Home right here in Marion, and with so many coming from out of town, we thought it easiest to have everything right there on the same day. The visitation, the service, and the catered lunch, were immediately followed by a full military burial at Cedar

Memorial Cemetery in Cedar Rapids. I had recorded my Sweet Adeline's quartet who sang "The Lord's Prayer", and Joyce sang "Amazing Grace". Our youngest granddaughter, Samantha, spoke about her special relationship with her grandpa.

I know it was exactly what Don would have wanted. In the weeks following, we had a tree planted in his honor at Lowe Park right here in uptown Marion, and it is comforting for us to be able to see it whenever we want. We also had a cement bench made and placed at the Marion golf course (near hole 5), inscribed with the words, "In honor of Don Bean who had 2 holes in one on this course", and below it, Don's favorite saying when he came home from golfing on a hot day, "There's always a breeze on the golf course".

In the days and weeks that followed, the reality began to sink in that I was on my own. After sixty-two years together and twenty one years growing up, you can imagine how alone I felt, especially every morning when I woke up. Even now, I still talk to myself in my head, "Well, you'd best get up now. No one else is here that requires you to do anything." I know I would have felt totally lost and adrift if it hadn't been for my dear friends, but most especially for my family. Even with DeLana's focus on the lives of her three daughters, and a growing number of grandchildren of her own, she always took time for me, and it has been Diane, who, through these many years, has become my "rock" and constant companion.

Several folks suggested that, living on my own, I should consider moving to a senior housing complex, but I quickly dismissed the idea. Don and I had wisely moved to a condominium where so much of the major care and upkeep of our house is taken care of. I felt confident that I could do the rest. This became abundantly clear as the years passed and my caring neighbors stepped up to look out for me in so many ways, great and small, from dropping off a meal to a phone call, like I so often get on an icy morning, warning me not to walk outside to get the paper until the ice melts.

My dear condo neighbors who are always looking out for me, Pat and John Hancock.

I don't know if there's a "secret" to a long marriage, but I know what worked to hold Don and I together. I believe the foundation of our relationship was built on our similar backgrounds both growing up on a farm, living simply and frugally, as well as both our families' involvement in a church community. We also shared a love for working with children in our careers, and a deep commitment to family.   In our younger days, I will never forget the many hours we spent on the dance floor. Throughout our marriage, we also enjoyed

175

playing cards with friends and neighbors, and of course, our many traveling adventures.

On top of the World Trade Center-1996

One of our most memorable trips was in 1996, when we went on a two-car joint family vacation with Diane, DeLana, Steve, and young daughters Ashley, Megan, and Samantha, on a long road trip east. We first stopped to visit our nephew, Greg Hopton and his wife, Lisa and their three boys, in Michigan, and then headed to Niagara Falls in New York. But of course, everything didn't go as planned when Steve's car was broken into at the motel, taking their suitcases! We drove on to Connecticut to stay with my sister, Joyce, and her husband, Paul, where DeLana and Steve went shopping to have enough clothes to see them through the rest of the trip! We continued on to visit Boston and Washington D.C., and since insurance eventually reimbursed for the stolen clothes, it all ended well!

Another trip that sticks in my mind is when, in October of 2004, Don and I traveled to England, to stay with Joyce and Paul, who were living there for a year for his consulting work building nuclear submarines. Now, it wasn't the first time we'd been out of the country since we'd taken a European tour back in 1984, seeing ten countries in twenty-one days, but this was a chance for us to experience things up close. We actually met Joyce and Paul in Ireland, touring there first, before taking the ferry across the Irish Sea and driving back to their flat in northern England. Picture the little cobbled village of Ulverston, chartered as a market town in 1280, where they were living.

While Paul was working, Joyce had gotten quite involved in the community, making daily visits to the town library, working out at the Leisure Center (a workout gym), and shopping at the outdoor market twice a week just down the street. Joyce and I share a love of singing, so I had fun going with her to rehearsals with the local women's chorus. We were also both teachers, so I accompanied her to the elementary school where she regularly volunteered. I was amazed that the elementary school had a whole school assembly every morning (without a peep from the students sitting on the gymnasium floor!) that included a Bible scripture and a prayer. Something not allowed in a public school in this country!

Since the refrigerator in their flat was tiny, Joyce went to the local grocery store every other day, and what an experience that was for me! Booth's grocery store had its own bus that had a regular route around the village, at no charge, that Joyce and I took, but on one of the days, we were a little late getting checked out to get back on the bus. Fortunately, the driver waited for us when we frantically waved our arms for him to stop!

While we were there, we also visited Wales and Scotland, driving to see so many little villages along the hilly, narrow, and winding roads. Keep in mind that Paul was accustomed to driving on the left side of the road, so he did all the driving while we were there. Every year, I still hang a special Christmas ornament of the Twelve Days of Christmas that Joyce bought for us at one of the quaint little shops. We ended our vacation in Edinburg (pronounced Edin-borough there), Scotland, taking a fabulous bus tour through the city, including the famous Edinburg Castle.

Of course, Don and I found great joy spending time with our granddaughters, Ashley, Megan, and Samantha, who, by the year 2000 were in high school. Without the loving parenting of DeLana and Steve, I know they wouldn't have become the successful, caring women they are today. I saw how both DeLana and Steve were intently focused on providing the best for their girls. Steve had worked his way up the managerial ladder at HyVee in order to provide a stable and comfortable home for the family. DeLana stayed home with the girls when they were growing up so she could spend quality time with them, only returning to teaching art when they were all in school.

Ashley is the eldest child, and to Don's delight, was a stand-out in every type of athletics she tried, although she was, and still is, never one to draw attention to herself. She was a star basketball player in high school, as well as tennis, continuing tennis while she was an undergraduate at Coe College. As Don liked to describe her, Ashley was also a "natural" at golf, even to this day. She received a Master's of Business Administration from the University of Iowa. After college, she landed a job as a Director of Marketing and Communications, eventually becoming the Chief Marketing Officer for The Wittern Group in Des Moines. Sadly, Don did not live to know her two beautiful daughters, Avery and Logan.

Megan is their middle child, and has also grown into an accomplished young woman. In high school, Megan also played basketball and tennis while still excelling academically. She also attended Coe College, venturing to New York City on her own for her internship there. Megan began her successful career at Wells Fargo in Des Moines, where she met her husband, Greg Levenhagen, both receiving their Master's degrees from the University of Iowa program for professionals. They have three sweet children, Joben, Kauri, and Natalie. Joben was the first-born great-grandchild and the only one who got to know Don and shares his middle name.

Like her older sisters, Samantha excelled in high school basketball, as well as volleyball, but in other ways set a unique course for herself. She bravely spent five weeks studying in Costa Rica for college credit. She showed her poise and creativity in becoming Iowa's representative for the title of Miss Czech Slovak twice. Samantha received a BA in Elementary Education from Iowa State University in Ames, her dad's alma mater, beginning her career as a teacher for non-English speaking students. She subsequently earned Master's degrees in ELL (English Language Learning), Learning and Technology, and Administration. She recently began a new venture introducing educators to an innovative teaching model that she co-founded. She now lives here in Marion with husband, Brock Dykes, and her three delightful children, Boston, Cannon, and Sophia.

It is these wonderful memories with Don that sustain me now, of the many times we enjoyed dancing, socializing, traveling, and spending time with family, but it is also important to me to reflect on how we navigated through the difficult times. Our marriage was not perfect, but I think it's the nature of life to have "ups and downs". I believe that the key to our long life together was a sense of commitment that we shared. Our marriage wasn't always smooth sailing, but we were both determined that we would work through the tough times.

But I think, equally as important as the things that we enjoyed together, was the support we gave each other in pursuing our individual dreams and passions. I think particularly of Don's sporting activities, whether it be golf, bowling, or attending team games. Don encouraged me in so many ways, joining Sweet Adelines, singing in our church choir, directing our children's choir, and Granny Basketball. I will forever be grateful for the way I was able to grow as an individual, especially now after Don's death, as I begin this next chapter of my life on my own.

Dressed in antique clothes for our 50th anniversary

1979

Chapter 18
On My Own

After Don died in 2017, I had to rethink my life, now as a single person. I hadn't thought about it before, but in many ways, it's a couple's world. Thankfully, during our marriage, I had developed interests apart from Don. A couple of years before he died, our first great grandchild, Joben, was born, and I was honored when his mother, Megan, asked if I would make a crib quilt for him. It took me all winter to embroider the fabric, but then I could not find anyone to quilt it for me. My mother, long gone, had always been the quilter of the family, but I decided to try to quilt it myself. After all, I'd sewed and done crafting all my life!

Unfortunately, I couldn't make it look right, so friends told me there were now sewing machines made specifically for quilting. That sounded like the solution for me, but I was shocked at the price! How could I justify something so expensive?! My family persuaded me that I'd worked all my life, and that now in my retirement years, I was entitled to buy it for myself, so I did! And what a joy my miracle machine has been for me, as I continue to spend countless hours creating so many quilted items, including several quilts for each of my eight great-grandchildren. I still take classes to this day on different ways of using the machine, including making table runners, placemats, etc!

Although I officially retired from teaching in 1995, I continued to do substitute teaching at the elementary school level for the next twenty-four years, in all grades, including special education, music, art, physical education, and counseling. Children were and still are a great source of joy for me. Even today, at age eighty-nine, I enjoy volunteering in the local schools in any way I can.

My church family continues to sustain me, as I have served in so many ways over the years – deacon, elder, children's church school teacher, and later, church school chairman, as well as many other committees. But again, it is through music that I've found the greatest satisfaction, not just singing in the church choir, but also participating in our bell choir. I combined my love of music and working with children when I directed our Cherub Choir for over ten years, which included children from kindergarten through second grade. Truly little angels!

I've also found more time to volunteer at the Granger House in Marion as well as the Marion Heritage Center, giving tours and talking about local history to visitors, much of which is reminiscent of my long-ago days growing up on the farm. I feel like I'm keeping that connection to the past alive for us older folks, as well as passing on an awareness of how it was in the old days to younger folks.

From Left: Don, Me, Byron Tabor, Nancy Domer, Emil Koval, George Domer, Mel Holubar and Norm Wright from the Marion Sunriser's Kiwanis Club

I've continued my active participation in our local Marion Sunrisers Kiwanis Club. Our club joined other local Kiwanis clubs in organizing a softball league for handicapped children that we called the Miracle League, providing not only the playing field, but the equipment and uniforms. Our Kiwanis group is particularly special to me since Don was a co-founder of our group fifty years ago. Just this year, I organized our fiftieth anniversary celebration which was a great success, although I wonder about our group's future, as our members are growing older like me.

Fund-raising is a big part of all these organizations. One of the most memorable of our fundraisers was when we were paid to advertise a mattress sale. We members stood outside at Lindale shopping plaza, each of us "wearing" a mattress with only our heads sticking out the top and our arms out the sides, waving and smiling at the passing cars! Don and I actually did this on several different occasions, so silly and so much fun, and all the while earning money to help families!

It goes without saying that my singing continues to bring me joy beyond church choir, through Sweet Adelines. Again, it's not just the singing that I enjoy, but the friendships I've gained over the years, connecting in different ways. In fact, it was a friend from Sweet Adelines who approached me at one of our rehearsals and asked if I had played basketball in my youth. And so that is how my involvement in the newly formed

Granny Basketball League began. I joined the Curvaceous Chicks team from Center Point, Iowa, (just north of Marion) in 2005, introducing me to a world of fun!

Now I'm only average height, and was certainly not a star basketball player in high school, but I had enjoyed playing then. Here was a chance for me to participate again, but in a little different way. The first requirement is that you had to be over fifty years old, although most players were much older, as I was seventy-two when I started! The league was organized following women's basketball rules of 1920, which means no running, touching, or jumping was allowed, if you can imagine! You could only dribble the ball twice before you had to pass the ball, and only the forwards could shoot a basket. The floor was divided in three sections.

We wore uniforms from that era, white long sleeve blouses and black bloomers that had to meet our knee-high stockings, so only our faces and hands were allowed to show. The color of our stockings was the only thing that distinguished one team from the other. My granddaughters forever tease me about the time I got a foul because I had "too much skin showing"! Somehow one of my stockings had slipped down a little, showing a bit of my knee! How scandalous!!!

We even played against the Harlem Globetrotters!

I felt like a kid again, having so much fun, but we were serious about winning our games! We had regular practices and a schedule of games, even tournaments, while also participating in city events including parades. As the camaraderie grew among us players, our bonds of friendship deepened. My sister, Joyce, recalls that one evening while she and her husband, Paul, were watching NBC national news in Connecticut, they were shocked to see me there on their TV with my team, in a news feature showcasing Granny basketball in the Midwest!

I stopped playing after thirteen years, but only for health considerations. In June of 2018, a year after Don died, I suddenly had terrible pains going up from the left side of my neck to the top of my head. I drove myself to the doctor. He insisted I go directly to the hospital, over my protests that I needed to go home first. Following his orders, I drove myself directly to the hospital (what, he didn't call an ambulance?!), where doctors there told me I had a blood clot covering the whole left side of my brain. They said it was so large that it was about to push my brain out of my skull! They called it a subdural hematoma, and for the first time, I was really afraid that I might die.

I had two options: they could drill a hole in my skull to drain it, or I could attempt to get it to shrink away myself. I chose the latter method, drinking at least six glasses of water each day, focusing on healthy eating, avoiding stressful situations, and exercising every day. I did all of that and more. I had a CT scan every few weeks to assess its growth, but after two months, there was no change. Finally, after five long months, it was gone! That regimen for healthy living had done the trick, and I've continued to follow it to this day.

Don with Senator Bob Dole and DeLana on the Honor Flight

Don had been gradually slowing down in his later years, so he was less inclined to take long trips, although he made the veteran's trip to Washington D.C. with DeLana on the "Honor Flight" in 2015. Don had served in the Korean War and had stayed in the Army reserves his entire life, retiring as Lieutenant Colonel, and as such, he was invited to join other veteran's to be honored for his service. DeLana was the one who encouraged him to go, serving as his official "guardian" for the trip. It was such a special time for them both as she had been his little shadow when she was small. And what a great time they had!

As Don was now staying closer to home, Diane and I began taking some vacations together (with Don's blessing, of course), beginning in 1997 with an Alaskan Cruise. Diane had never married, so it was natural that the two of us were drawn to taking joint ventures. I'd never been on a cruise before, so it was quite an adventure, but going with Diane made it so special for me!

I was most amazed at the sight and the deafening sound of the glaciers along the Alaskan coast as they crashed into the water. We happened to be there on July 4th, watching the fireworks from our ship, a memorable sight, as you can imagine! The hardest part was keeping each other awake since the fireworks didn't start until midnight when it got dark enough! We enjoyed many ports of call, touring Denali Park, and while visiting the capital city of Juneau, we learned that the only way to get there was by plane or boat, since there was no access by land. For that reason, many people owned their own private seaplane, using water runways at their airport. Touring the city of Anchorage, we noticed the huge flowers growing because it rarely gets completely dark during their summers. The tour guide told us that the opposite is true in winter, when it is dark for much of the time, causing a spike in mental issues among the people there.

Kangaroo

In 2013, Diane and I repeated our adventuring, but this time, we flew to Australia and New Zealand for fifteen days, living on a cruise ship once we got there. Of course, while onboard the cruise ship, I sang in the ship's chorus, performing on the last day. I remember how the mountainsides were filled with sheep. We visited the Tasmania Animal Reserve, getting up close with a koala bear, the kangaroos, bears, cockatoos, and an emu. We even got to dance with the native Māori Warriors. We also toured the iconic Sidney Opera House and saw the fiords in Australia, with everything so green and lush! We did so much walking, up and down their steep, hilly sidewalks.

The people listened to our ship's chorus sing where ever they could find a spot.

Because Diane and I were both teachers, we shared a particular interest in Reading Recovery that had been coming out of New Zealand. A friend of Diane's was a teacher there, so we were able to spend a day at her school. It stands out in my memory that the students there all wore large brimmed hats outdoors to keep from getting sunburned. They told us that they are under a hole in the ozone layer, and in great danger if they get more than fifteen minutes of sun. Also unusual for elementary education, the schools there all had swimming pools, where the teachers (not assistants) taught swimming lessons. Surprisingly, the teachers said they took the students camping in the mountains each year, something unheard of in the states.

The students eating lunch at the school we visited in New Zealand. Notice that they are all wearing hats. Everyone had to bring their own lunch.

It has been a blessing that Don and I had decided, in March of 2008, to move to a condominium, since it was becoming clear that Don was no longer able to keep up with the outdoor work. Our new place is perfect for me now as a single person, with just enough work to keep me busy, but no more shoveling, mowing, or heavy maintenance work to do!

Just when everything seemed to have settled, my world, like everyone else's, was changed by the Covid pandemic. We were told not to leave our homes much, but if you had to go out in public, to stay six feet apart, wear a mask, and get back home as soon as possible. No large gatherings, certainly not outside your immediate family. It was a scary time when so many folks feared they would lose their sanity, being so isolated, without getting together with friends.

It was during this time, that Diane and I cemented our tie as a "family unit" that DID NOT isolate from each other during those terrible times. I learned just how essential human contact is to our well-being, something we just took for granted in the past! Thankfully, our lives have pretty much returned to normal now, but there are still cases of Covid around, and we're careful to get regular boosters. Will we ever be completely rid of masks?!

Diane and I would go to Ashley and Dorrie's house on Sunday afternoon and watch Logan and Avery until Thursday while their parents worked at home during Covid.

During Avery and Logan's naptimes, we would often go to Megan and Greg's house (who lived about 10 minutes from Ashley) to play UNO, do "schoolwork", and other fun things with Kauri and Joben. We often stayed for supper.

On Friday mornings, we would go to Samantha and Brock's house to play with Boston and Cannon and do learning activities. This weekly schedule lasted from December 2020-June 2021!

My two daughters are like the bookends of my life. Diane and I continue to be close companions, our lives overlapping in many ways, which is a joy and a particular blessing to me since I'm no longer keen to drive long distances. DeLana has always been our family organizer, bringing all of us, including my precious great-grandchildren, together for so many fun gatherings and activities. There's never a dull moment when she's around! I am indeed blessed!Chapter 19

Chapter 19
What's It All About?

So, what is life really all about? You'd think I'd have all the answers after nearly ninety years! I think of the lyrics from Burt Bacharach's song from the sixties.

What's it all about, Alfie?

Is it just for the moment we live?

What's it all about when you sort it out, Alfie?

Are we meant to take more than we give

Or are we meant to be kind?

I don't pretend to be all-wise, but I'd like to share some insights I've gained along the way. Yes, I think we are meant to be kind. The frame of reference that has stood the test of time for me is to be a giver, not a taker, in life. Henry Ford, considered by many to be one of the most successful men in the world, is quoted as saying, *"To do more for the world than the world does for you — that is success"*. Winston Churchill once said, *"We make a living by what we get, but we make a life by what we give."*

My parents instilled the Golden Rule in me from the time I was small and "treating others the way I would like to be treated" has been a guidepost throughout these many years. This ancient rule has been stated in different ways in all the major world religions, and seems so simple, and yet it is apparently not so easy to follow in practice. I must admit that we're less inclined to be kind to someone that doesn't look or act like us, or doesn't share our world view, but that's a bigger discussion for another time.

I believe that it's the simple acts of kindness that matter most, a helping hand, a kind word, or even just a smile, especially to someone we might not have given much thought. My spiritual life has helped to stay me on the path, although I have sometimes fallen short, especially when someone doesn't share my opinion of things! But overall, I'd like to think that my life has made a difference for good. That was my mother's barometer of success, not how much money a person made, but the degree to which someone's life made this earth a better place.

I remember the "angels" who made a difference in my life, selflessly giving of themselves to get me through the rough times, sometimes when they barely knew me. Such was the case with Dr. Almazov, who offered to tutor me in college Spanish, week after week, at a time when I thought there was no hope for me to get through it. My words of thanks just didn't seem like enough, but he wouldn't accept any money for the hours he helped me.

At another juncture in my life, back when I was in the early years of my teaching career in Dysart, a more experienced teacher, Sylvia Heckroth, took me under her "angel" wing. She is the one I leaned on when I needed advice or help, and it was Sylvia who I turned to when I was afraid that I was going to miscarry with my first child. She was always there for me.

Much later in my career, as a veteran teacher, I had just moved to a new school where I didn't know anyone, which turned out to be my loneliest year of teaching. The other teachers there were a tight-knit group, and I just didn't seem to fit in with them. It was an old friend, Barb Null, who came to my rescue. She and I had taught together at my previous school, and she somehow sensed that I felt alone. She never failed to call me every week and knew just what to say to lift my spirits!

Sometimes, we may not even realize we need it, when we get a boost from someone in a different way. Near the end of my teaching career, another "angel" appeared in my life, not to get me through a difficult time, but rather to push me to realize my full potential. Dr. Ross was a department head in the Cedar Rapids school system, and he singled me out to encourage me to go beyond my classroom work, to become a teacher of teachers. I was unsure that I could take that step, but he always said, "You're the expert!".

I hesitated at first to single out these four caring folks, knowing that I have left out the names of so many others that have impacted my life, but I felt I should give specific examples of special people. They continue to inspire me to be like them, and so I try to keep passing kindness forward,

making the world a better place for everyone. Who could hope for anything more?! If my life has shown me anything, it is that the best way to find happiness for yourself, is to bring happiness to others.

This picture was in the Cedar Rapids Gazette when the girls nominated me for Granny Smith in 1998

Disappointingly, kindnesses aren't always noticed, but I think we all appreciate recognition sometimes, so I try to be generous with my words of thanks. I've been fortunate to receive many awards during my life, but recognition is most meaningful to me when I'm taken completely by surprise. In 1998, my three granddaughters, Ashley, Megan, and Samantha, entered me in the national Granny Smith contest in Washington State. It was enough of an honor that they nominated me, but I even won in our Iowa region and placed

third in the country! Then in 2013, I was recognized by the people of our town when they voted me Marion's Citizen of the Year. Again, something I never expected.

Norm Wright from the Marion Sunrisers Kiwanis presenting me with the Marion Citizen of the Year 2000 plaque.

But truly, my most valued recognition was when my family created a special award for me, surprising me by naming me the "Energizer Bunny". They presented me with a stuffed Energizer Bunny and each wrote something about me, which so warmed my heart! Following are excerpts of their loving words.

Feb, 2019

The

Energizer

Bunny Award

Your energy and enthusiasm to take on any challenge is inspiring!

Here are some of the reasons you were chosen for this award!

"Your never-ending energy and drive to help others is so inspiring and the world is a better place with you in it". Megan and family

"Through your many activities you make a positive difference in the lives of so many people, often in ways which may not be apparent in the moment". Ashley and family

"Very few people in the world get to experience all that I have with my grandma. You're just way cooler than every other grandma!" Samantha and family

"Your energy benefits so many others because of the unselfish ways you dedicate your time. Your example will always inspire me!" DeLana

"You are an inspiration to all, an example to emulate, doubtless anyone of us could duplicate." Steve

"You inspire me to always keep going and never give up!" Diane

And so, I accept the mantle of Energizer Bunny, because I am indeed determined about life, rarely giving up on myself or anyone else! But again, it has been with the help of others that I've been able to do this throughout my life. I've also learned that I do better in life in partnership with another person, rather than on my own. My enduring marriage with Don enabled me to work through so many difficult times.

And now, on my own, Diane is a big part of my life, seeing me through the loneliness of Covid isolation, and even today, as my constant companion. DeLana and Steve, and my granddaughters and their families, are also a central part of my world, including me in every family activity and right there whenever I need help. My life is richer, too, because of my extended family, especially my only surviving sibling, Joyce and daughter Carolyn, as well as my cousins ("sisters"), Mary and Betty. But I would be adrift without my dear friends and neighbors. I have so much to be thankful for!

In 2010, I got one of the biggest surprises of my life, a phone call from the father of one of my second-grade students, asking me if I was the teacher who taught his daughter at Hiawatha School in Cedar Rapids in 1978. He explained that his grown daughter, Melissa Louvar Reeves, was coming to visit Cedar Rapids and wanted to see me and present me with a book she had written, "Building Sustainable Leadership Capacity". Her mother had in fact been one of my parent volunteers when I taught Melissa back when she was in second grade.

Melissa and her mother visited me a few weeks after her father's phone call when she handed me her book and showed me what she had written about me. I found out then that I had been an "angel" at a critical time in her young life! She went on to get a double major in psychology and special education with an emphasis in behavioral disorders. Below is a portion of the quote from her book.

> "As I write about what I have accomplished, I must emphasize that I could not have done any of this without the support of others. Mrs. Bean, my second-grade teacher, was one of the first who changed my life. This little second-grade girl, who loved to learn, had shut down – not only in class, but with reading at home. My previous teacher had made me feel like I had failed. My mom tried coaxing me to read, yet I was silent.
>
> Somehow my mom convinced me to talk about what had happened in first grade. I had been put down after reading. My mom talked to the principal. She asked him to put me in the best second-grade teacher's class in school. Mrs. Bean believed in me, re-instilled my love for learning and reading, and told me that I could do anything. She was patient in helping me overcome my fears and encouraged me when I was hesitant. I firmly believe that I would not have received a college degree, let alone a doctorate, if it were not for Mrs. Bean.

Once I learned how to read and gained in confidence, you could not get me to put a book down. That is true, yet today. [My collection of books] symbolize how much I overcame my frustrations, with the support and encouragement of one teacher, Mrs. Bean. I never forgot that experience of being helped and how it saved me!"

Melissa still keeps in touch with me even with her busy schedule as Dr. Reeves. She travels throughout the United States giving presentations, helping children and families, and has co-authored three other books. When she was in Cedar Rapids giving a presentation to a large audience, she invited her mother and me to sit in the front row. To my surprise, she introduced us to everyone there in the auditorium! If I had had buttons on my shirt, they would have all popped off!

When I see my reflection in the mirror now, I wonder where that little farm girl went! I know I don't look the same today with my white hair and wrinkles, but I still feel the same inside, not always sure of myself, but always willing to try most anything. And although my personality is still basically the same, my ideas about life continue to evolve. I hope that my life's story has given you something to think about.

At the end of the day, I leave you with a challenge, and that is to continually grow your empathetic heart. I've learned that "putting myself in someone's else's shoes" enables me to connect with someone, even someone who may be very different from myself. Maybe, just maybe, if we can see things from another's perspective, and understand how they think and feel, this world will become a kinder, gentler place.

Hopefully, my story has given you an understanding of a mid-western country girl's view on life who grew up in a world without diversity. Lone Tree was a somewhat isolated farm community where there were no people of color. Abusive marriages and unwed mothers were rarely spoken of, and I'd never heard of homosexuality. Opportunities for women outside the home were limited. My background and experiences may be very different from yours, but in the end, we share our humanity and our will to make things better. Maybe that is, indeed, what it's all about!

The whole family in 2022

2008

MEMORIES OF DONNA

From CATHY CONLEY,
my Principal at Arthur Elementary School:

I met you my first year as a principal. It was your last year before your retirement. I admired you right away, after our first teacher's meeting at Arthur! At that meeting I had asked the staff some questions about ideas for our year. No one had any comments. The staff was very quiet during the whole meeting. I was puzzled. Right after the meeting you came to my office. You explained to me that the previous principal never listened to our comments and would even get upset whenever teachers tried to give her input. So, we were all used to just listening and doing what she wanted. You told me to "Hang in there. The staff would soon learn you did indeed want our input and wanted us to get involved with ideas." So, you helped me so much, to understand my new staff. You were always there to do whatever needed to get done. You would change grade levels when it was needed. You helped me in my first principal's job!

From SHIRLEY WATKINSON KING, childhood friend:

I remember the ice skating parties at our creek, especially since my parents went all out to make them a success. In those days we had ice skates that just clamped onto the bottom of our shoes. Dad built a huge bonfire and my mother baked a cake to pass around. I also remember our attempts at gymnastics during noon hours in the school yard. They were rather lame but we did not do too badly. They were not medal worthy, but such fun!

One night you and I stayed at Mary Ann Lorack's home. We were supposed to fix Duane (her brother) something to eat since their parents were gone for the evening. We made him a toasted cheese sandwich. Real cooks! We slept on the floor because they were remodeling their home. You and I also stayed overnight with Nina Lavely once. I think it may have been her birthday. I remember selling apples and popcorn during basketball games and walking home together. You stayed with your Aunt Laura Schuessler. I stayed with my cousin and family, further down the street. We had many profound conversations!

I remember going home with you on the school bus. Your parents were so kind and made me always feel so comfortable. You always had your chores to do. I watched you iron bedding and clothes on your big mangle, a huge electric machine that would iron large things straight. Your parents hosted lots of card parties. They had one the evening that I stayed. We went to your room and talked and giggled A LOT. You were probably (whether you liked it or not) my best friend in high school. You were loyal, kind and thoughtful and still are today. Love, always.

From SARAH MCCAW, friend from church:

Thank you for being a mentor for our confirmation students. It is so important for our youth to have adult friends at their church.

From GENNY KEDROVSKY, friend:

I used to visit you and Don often when Diane and DeLana
were small. They always read a bedtime book together.
When I was there, they allowed me to read the bedtime book
with the girls. I loved that. We had many great times
together. I taught at Wright School with Don. I moved to
Minnesota when the girls were around eight and ten. God has
truly gifted you in many wonderful ways. You have shared
your beautiful gift of singing all your life. Your family shows
numerous examples of what your precious hands have made.
Your example of caring, thoughtfulness, and constantly giving
to others is contagious. What a blessing to have you as my
dear friend these many years. Much love.

From SUE STOCK ANTHONY, childhood neighbor and long-time friend:

I have known you and your family since I was a young girl.
Your family were very good neighbors and special friends to
my family. We both lived on farms northeast of Lone Tree,
Iowa. While I was growing, you were a "Nanny" to my
brothers and I. You stayed with us at times, even catching the
school bus from our home. Our friendship continues to grow
through your wedding to Don, the growing up years of your
daughters (Diane and DeLana) and yet today. We get together
with Betty and Mary.

We have our careers of teaching elementary grades in
common. When I began teaching, we spent many hours on
the phone. You were like a mentor to me, giving me advice or
reassurance many times. I also took your Math Their Way

week-long workshop. It was a good, educational week! You had so many great ideas. You worked endless hours in and out of school. I valued your ideas, opinions and suggestions, as they helped me to grow into the teacher that I am today. Our friendship continues to grow. You will always have a special place in my heart.

From DR. LORI DINGMAN, my eye doctor and friend:

Thank you so much for the lovely quilt gift! I love that you made it. I will think of you every year when I put it out. You are such an incredible lady. I am so grateful that God put you in my path! Thank you for all of the wonderful visits over the years. I look forward to many more!

From ELLEN HEALEY, Sweet Adelines friend:

I so much appreciated singing with you in Cedar Sounds! You have a very lovely voice and I could tell you really understood the barbershop style. I was blessed to be a part of the chorus. It seems like you had many great times! Thank you for your continued kindness. Love, Ellen

From GERI HASLEY, 3rd grade teacher when I taught at Arthur School, Cedar Rapids:

I value you as a good work partner. Just the way I think of us yet, now in retirement. I was happy to hear you say that you valued me as a good work partner too. We had fun and worked productively together. We both cherish children and understand that the legacy we leave is a proud and loving one. We both changed classrooms often but we were lucky to be right beside each other for several years. Those were the best years. We laughed and cried together. Our students worked so well together. Your first graders worked many times with my slower third graders, giving them a good feeling of helping other students. We often met after school to share cheerful family news, much cheaper and more helpful than visits to the psychiatrist!

You were the most generous and organized person I ever knew. Your killer schedule was unbelievable. Most of it revolved around music and church work and always your cherished family. You were fun to be with. But I most liked that I always learned from you. Paul and I have been married fifty-three years. I can fully understand your great loss of your strong, Don. Both of you were a model, about family and fun. You traveled a lot to complete your journey together. I love our lunches together in retirement. You and yours are in my prayers. Thank you for the "Angel of Friendship."

From JANET WALKER, Sweet Adelines friend:

Donna Bean is the original "Energizer Bunny". Those who know her know that she thrives on being involved and being busy. And, best of all, she volunteers to help instead of waiting to be asked! This has been true of the 46 years she was involved in her Sweet Adeline's Chorus. Donna is an asset to any group she is involved. Thanks, Donna, for sharing all of your talents!

From JO BADER, Sweet Adelines friend:

Donna has been a great friend through our 40+ years of Sweet Adeline's. I always knew I could count on her to get together to make costumes. We walked/ran around London doing 40 walk steps and 40 run steps—her idea. We did lots of money-making projects. We only wished that someone would have told us we couldn't pick dandelions (for wine) until the sun came up. Thanks, Donna, for lots of good memories....

From KATHY BURNS, Sweet Adelines friend:

June 13, 2008 is a date most Cedar Rapids folks will not forget. The Cedar River crested at 31.2 feet. Ten square miles (14%) of the city was affected. The previous record flood was 20 feet set in 1929 and 1951. Unfortunately, my home was flooded, 3.5 feet of water on the first floor. What a mess! So appreciative of my Sweet Adeline's chorus, Cedar Sounds, when they came to help. Donna was a member of the chorus. She spent three days working nonstop helping to clean up. She even took items home to wash. I am very grateful.

From JUDY CHAPMAN, friend and organist at the First Presbyterian Church:

When you took charge of our Cherub choir, it was a large boisterous group of youngsters, sometimes as many as 20 young children. The little singers always delighted the congregation in worship, in their white robes and big red bows. Your energy and patience were endless, and your sewing skills were also put to good use! I remember how much they liked the impromptu parades with their noisy instruments, followed by a treat from the gumball machine. Although you attempted to 'retire' many times, we could always coax you back in a pinch. The highlights of the year were Palm Sunday (with the waving palms) and of course the Christmas Pageant. Thank you for so many happy memories!

From MARILYN FAIRCHILD, Cedar Sounds Sweet Adelines Chorus Director and friend:

Thank you for all of your years of dedication to this wonderful chorus. I don't think there is a thing you did not take on over your 46 years. So many good times, so many memories. Your enthusiasm has never waned. You have always been ready to volunteer to do whatever needed to be done. Keep active and we will see you when we get our lunches going! In harmony.

From DR. MELISSA LOUVAR REEVES, once a shy little girl in my 2nd grade classroom. Her story is in my book:

I am so glad you are writing your life story! You played such a huge role in my life. I share our story often! I am honored to have you write our story. I only have one condition. I want a copy of your book. I am on a plane most weeks doing training all over the country in school crisis prevention through recovery and meeting the mental health needs of students and staff. Rewarding work, but exhausting. We know educators are strong, resilient and amazing. We keep focusing on the positive and leaning on each other to make it through hard times. Keep doing your awesome work and stay healthy.

From PAT HENRY, Sweet Adelines friend:

Hi Donna! Well, I have known you 10 years and got to sing with you ten years in Cedar Sounds Chorus. You are a delightful lady, full of pep, energy, well anyway on Tuesday nights at chorus you were. Always ready to get on the risers and sing, sing, sing. Or even putting up the risers to get the rest of us ready to join in. Even though tired, or maybe not always wanting to be there because of a long day at school teaching or whatever...you always gave your very best. There were competitions, shows, luncheons, singing at different churches.....wow what a great 10 years with you! What fun! I just want to thank you for being such a good friend all these years and I thank God for your friendship! Thanks Donna! God Bless you!

From BETTY MALONE HOLLOWAY, cousin, raised with us – like sisters:

I was five when Mary and I moved in with Donna's family. She was busy in high school. Joanne and Marvin were about grown up and on their own. I remember you playing high school basketball, playing the piano, and singing. Your voice was so good and beautiful. We drove to Davenport to watch you sing for Ted Mack's talent hour on TV. I was so excited for you.

It was fun to watch when your dates came to pick you up: LaVonn Crawford, Bob Carter, Oscar Weir, and Don Bean. I thought you looked like a princess. When you began teaching and came home on weekends, I loved to help you correct papers. I loved it when you asked Mary and I to serve punch and coffee at your wedding reception. It was fun to play with your babies and push them in Joyce's doll buggy. I loved hearing my older sister sing and play the piano. As a result, I love the 40's music. You sang at all of the weddings and funerals. You have always been a joy in my life, Donna. I love you like an older sister.

From MARY ELLEN MALONE YOPP FUHRMEISTER, cousin raised with us – like sisters:

It is a joy to take a walk down memory lane with you, Donna (We had a long lane). I have great memories, but not a lot, as Donna was about to leave home at the time. I was six and Betty was five when we moved in with your family. Marvin and Joanne were about grown up and gone. Donna was busy in high school, church, 4-H and with friends. It was a wonder that she had time to date. I recall her dates coming to pick her up. LaVonn Crawford who was handsome and played in a small band came often. Bob Carter soon came often. Then, my favorite, Don Bean, began to come. He paid attention to Betty and I, teasing us. We looked forward to those dates. Donna reminded me of a movie star, all dolled up and pretty.

She made a big impact on me when she bought Betty and I new, almost matching, dresses for Easter. I can see them to this day hanging in the stairway waiting for the next person to take them upstairs. They were salmon colored out of light denim. I was tickled pink to have a store-bought dress. So sweet of you. Usually, we wore homemade dresses or hand – me-down ones. I did not mind. The dresses were just made differently.

When you came to visit, we loved pushing Diane in Joyce's doll buggy and playing with her. She was so cute. You sure have a nice family. I felt guilty later, one time. Your mom made a comment about you not being able to afford a new bra in your first year of teaching. She did not think you should buy some things that you did buy. At the time I wasn't a bit concerned. Still not! But looking back, I think your mom just needed someone to vent? Things she mentioned went in and out of my head. Some things stuck, like, "Pull a weed every time you see one!" Well – No more – I use my own head, as of lately. Donna – What a sweet, giving, lovely, cousin, that I was lucky enough to have shared your home with, in life! You are always perfect in my eyes!

From KAREN SCHUESSLER, niece, daughter of brother Marvin:

It is wonderful that you are writing a book. You have lived an active and interesting life. It is great to share your stories with others. I remember coming to your house, as a child. A high light was jumping on your basement trampoline. It was such fun! I also remember celebrating all of our birthdays together. Some memories of you and your family took place at Grandma and Grandpa's farm home. I was always so impressed with their large house. It has two stairways and all large rooms. I remember the closet in the south bedroom. I'll never forget all the fun I spent on the high tree swing. Grandpa would push me to make me go higher and higher. The cousins would play "Hide and Seek" with Joyce. There were so many great hiding places. They also had a little pool we would play in.

Now that we are grown up, I really enjoy seeing you and Diane in Iowa, and Joyce in Connecticut. You radiate joy and happiness. We always have so much to talk about! You inspire me with all of your energy and curiosity about the world. You are a gift to the people in your life as you are always learning something new and setting a great example to those around you.

From PAMELA DAYLE HOPTON JONES, niece, daughter of sister Joanne:

"The Lord searches every heart and understands every desire and every thought." I Chronicles 28:9. Thank you for your unconditional love that you have demonstrated throughout your lifetime. Praying for you and thanking the Lord for you. When our families were visiting so much during my growing up years, we always had the best times! Thank you for your delicious meals, your laughter, great crafts, beautiful quilts, your singing, sharing all of your teaching and wisdom!

You supported all of our little shows, always having time for our family and a special love and caring for others. Thank you for your labor of love, using Grandma Schuessler's quilt pieces for your "Covid" project. You turned them into so many different quilts. Such a legacy you gave each of us, that all began with Grandma's quilt pieces. You are appreciated and are surrounded by our love and prayers. God bless you! When my arms can't reach people who are close to my heart, I hug them with my prayers.

From GREGORY WAYNE HOPTON, nephew, son of sister, Joanne:

Here are some of my thoughts and memories of my Aunt Donna. Growing up in the 60's and 70's seemed to be simpler times – or maybe my childhood was just protected better than others. I was truly blessed with strong bonds connecting family.

Even though I did not realize it at the time, my memories and experiences with the Bean family formed who I am today with great impact. From my earliest memories as a young boy, I have vivid memories of being excited for the long trips to Iowa in our station wagon or the anticipation for Beans to arrive to our home in Ohio. When the families were together, it truly felt like one family that celebrated being together. Our time was not focused around the TV; but rather centered around activities like visiting the Glass Barn in Cincinnati, bowling, playing pool, going to the movies seeing The Sound of Music many times, enjoying Maid-Rite sandwiches, playing euchre, catching fireflies, and even the women went to the local Paul Dixon show in Cincinnati one Thanksgiving holiday.

Uncle Don always engaged with the kids by tickling us if we did not acknowledge the superiority of the Iowa Hawkeyes over the Ohio State Buckeyes. As a teacher, Aunt Donna interacted with us with planned activities and/or short trips – I especially enjoy the special messages that she would cook in the pancakes. Diane and Delana were like sisters to me. Every day that we were together was a new adventure. We would have club meetings, practice our lines for the upcoming play for our parents, play with the pet bunnies, jump on the trampoline in the basement, play boardgames, or play pool. Diane always wanted to understand what products that Ohio could produce other than Ohio Blue Tip Matches. Delana and I were always competitive in our games that we would play – I have to admit that she won most of the time.

The memories are many and the impact was great – I had ablessed childhood and the Bean family was a big part of that childhood.

From TERRI LEE HOPTON, niece, daughter of sister Joanne:

"You crown the year with your goodness, and your paths drip with abundance." (Psalms 65:11). I will never forget the time, at your home in Marion. I absolutely could not wait to get there. The hours we spent on your trampoline in the basement - unlimited! Then there were all of the July 4th parades we attended! Even now, when I go to a fourth of July celebration, I'm disappointed because it does not compare to my memories of them in Iowa! More Marion memories in that home – decorating cakes for Easter.... the purple and pink icing! Your rabbits inspired me to get rabbits of my own! One thing that frightened me to death was the tickle attacks from Uncle Don!!! Then, there was the famous "Humpty Dumpty" cement wall in your back yard. I loved that house...but I loved all of the memories at that house.

Then you moved to the "country". That was my favorite house because of the horses and creek fun. I still remember the horses A LOT – even remember riding with DeLana and getting chased by angry cows out in the pasture! Of course, how can I forget the mud slide down the bank into the creek! We were all covered completely in mud! You just calmly hosed us down and laughed along with us. One time

Greg and I were staying with all of you. All of us were going out to the farm to meet up with our parents. A lot of the roads were gravel and there wasn't air conditioning in any cars at that time. So we rode in your car with the windows all down. My long blonde hair was a tangled, matted mess when we got to the farm. My mom was furious – but you just laughed along with us as we were riding.

And the visits to Ohio – I couldn't wait until you all arrived!!! A memory that I have as a kid was being dragged to the "Glass Barn" and what seemed like a million craft stores with you and my mom. As an adult, I have incredible memories at the Glass Barn, which went out of business a few years ago. I always thought you were much nicer than my mom, but I think that is what Aunts are supposed to be! I have nothing but fond and happy memories of our trips to Iowa and your visits to Ohio. As a kid, I always wished we lived closer, but now that I'm older, I realize that being farther away from family made our visits that much more special. My work ethic, I definitely got from the Schuessler side of the family. I see so much of myself in my mom and my Aunt Donna!

From JOYCE CAROL SCHUESSLER WERDEN, younger sister and collaborator on this book:

I now realize there are only a handful of people who literally changed my life. In your case, Donna, you didn't so much change my life as you did SAVE it. We all have rough spots in our lives. No matter what happened, you were there for me. When I was growing up, you brought me up to stay with you when Mom was not there and I was feeling lost. You helped me with my 4-H projects so many times. When I was in college you were there to pick me up and spend the day with your family, although I messed up the connection some. I realized you had a sense of when I'd be upset (even when I didn't). I remember crying that first week of college. I guess you knew that would be hard.

After Carolyn was born, you could not come, but you sent Diane. She is an extension of you in so many ways. After my divorce we stayed with you for two weeks every summer. You took care of Carolyn and I slept late every day. You told me that I needed some rest. You knew! So many times and so many things.......I just wanted to say, "Thank you." I knew how emotional I would be to say it. I am writing it for myself and my needs. In any case, you have a special place in my heart. Love, Joyce.

From CAROLYN JOYCE WERDEN MERSHON, my niece, sister Joyce's daughter:

It is hard to narrow my many memories down. I spent many summer vacations in Iowa. They are memories that I will always cherish! You always made me feel so loved and comfortable in your home and always made extra effort to make sure I got to do all of the fun things I wanted to. Showbiz Pizza, parks garage sales, swimming, fireworks, endless games of Careers and watching all of the "shows" the girls and I would put on for you, are just a few things that come to mind. One of the things I remember most was you taking me to the grocery store as soon as I arrived and letting me pick out all of the fun, sugary foods and drinks my mom would never buy for me! Captain Crunch cereal was always on the list!

I always remember the first summer when my mom left and I was in Iowa two weeks without her for the first time. I was nervous and a little sad after we dropped her off at the airport, having never been away from her for that long. You took me to see Field of Dreams at the movie theater and it was just what I needed to make me feel better. From then on, I had a fantastic time and always looked forward to my times in Iowa, having you guys all to myself!

I'm sure you remember the year I was flying out to Iowa alone and there were tornado warnings in Illinois, where my connecting flight was. You and Diane waited at the airport for me for 8 hours before I finally arrived!!! Then, since my mom had arranged for the flight attendants to take care of getting me to where I needed to be, I had to wait with them until everyone else had gotten off the plane before one of them escorted me off. So, after 8 hours, you and Diane watched everyone else get off. I was nowhere in sight. You were thinking, after waiting all of that time, I wasn't on the flight. I did finally get off with the attendant. These are a few of my wonderful memories in Iowa!

From DIANE RENEE BEAN, older daughter:

There are so many important things that my mom and dad have taught me and inspired me to strive for. First of all is LOVE. There was never a time in my life that I didn't know that my parents loved me. Even at times when I'm sure that I completely frustrated them, I knew I was loved. Out of that came FRIENDSHIP. I always felt that I was lucky to have parents that were teachers because they knew how to talk to my friends and not embarrass me like so many of my friend's parents did. Since Dad passed away, I feel that my friendship

219

with Mom has deepened as we do more things together and spend more time together.

Another thing that I got from them was INDEPENDENCE. They always wanted to make sure that we were ready to face the world as adults and made sure that we had the skills that we needed. When I was nearing the end of my college life, I decided that I wanted to do some of my student teaching in England. I had my arguments ready and planned on getting a student loan to pay for it. I was surprised that they both thought it was a great idea! I spent eight weeks in the United Kingdom at a time when there weren't cell phones and it cost a dollar a minute to phone home. Needless to say, this taught me to figure things out for myself and not depend on my parents as much since I could only talk to them briefly about once a month.

I have also tried to emulate my mom in the area of HELPING OTHERS. She has always been involved in the community through Kiwanis, church, Sweet Adelines, the Heritage Center and volunteering and teaching in schools. She even had over 700 hours of volunteering at Linn Mar one year! I have tried to help others by being involved in church, schools, my reading council and Sweet Adelines. I think that it makes both of us feel like we are making a difference (and maybe making someone's life a little easier) if we can help out. Our many months together during COVID, when we went to Waukee during the week to help out Ashley's family, spent some afternoons with Megan's family and Friday mornings with Samantha's family, were some of the most special times that I have had!

Mom, you are one of the most special people that I have ever met and I am lucky to have known you!

From DELANA KAY BEAN HUBLER, younger daughter:

When I think about my years growing up, I think of the sum of so many wonderful experiences that left me with a strong foundation for life. This foundation's basic structure is made from values. I was raised with expectations and experiences that revolved around things like respect, responsibility, hard work, community, family, and compassion. I was given so many opportunities. Through these opportunities I was able to utilize these values and also learn so much about myself and abilities and possibilities for life as an adult.

If Diane or I showed an interest in something we were given the opportunity to give it a try. An example would be when I was young, I enjoyed building. I was given wood tools, a box of wood, and some instruction. From there I could just "create!" One of the first things I built on my own was a doghouse. I was so proud! When I carried it out to the patio to show my amazing creation it fell apart! I was so disappointed but had been taught about the value of the process of doing something. This process enables you to work hard, evaluate and improve even if you aren't initially successful. How many times have I relied on this process through my life? I remember all of the trips to the local ceramics shop or craft store with mom because I loved it! Becoming an art teacher was probably influenced from these adventures.

When I was in high school, I cooked dinner many times which I enjoyed. Thinking back about this I am sure I left plenty of kitchen messes and there were many meals that were not very edible as I learned but I was still given the opportunity and never was told something was bad or I was messy! I have always felt like I have some skill in many things because of these experiences. We were given the gift of **so** many opportunities. I felt like this was so valuable I wanted to pass down to my own children as a parent.

We always went on a family vacation. I got to see so many places and we have so many great family memories of those trips and hours in the car together. So many smiles from these trips. Through this opportunity I gained a love of travel, but I also gained a better vision of where and how others live.

I loved animals and the outdoors. One of my greatest gifts was moving to the country when I was twelve. Having horses and a big yard taught us a lot about hard work. But I also learned about working together as a family until the job was done and that some things that are so valuable are worth all of the hard work. In my adult life I have never been deterred by the amount of work involved to reach a goal, this was learned from my parents and time living in the country. Our neighborhood in the country also was like its own community - people helped each other and supported each other.

Mom and Dad were both very involved in the community. They were always willing to help others through their organizations. Diane was in college for the majority of my high school years, and they had time commitments between work and community involvement. These years taught me a lot about responsibility. I remember the first car I bought at a dealership when I was 18. Both parents had other commitments, so I had to go to the dealership and haggle with the salesman and purchase the car by myself. I was so nervous! I ended up with the car and this experience-built confidence for future situations in life where I might not feel comfortable. I still really dislike buying a car but am ready when I walk into the salesperson's office! When I turned sixteen, I drove to the driver's license office myself to get my license! :-) I am not sure if this taught me anything positive but looking back it is funny! I was given so many chances to learn responsibility – these experiences helped me as I began working and had my own family.

When making decisions growing up, I would always think about if my decision would disappoint my parents in any way. As a new parent, I remember thinking about this and wondering how my parents instilled this in me because they never verbally expressed this expectation. Their parenting style was through love and support. When my own kids were adults, they said they had this same feeling as they made decisions growing up! Success! □
As my own children were growing up, I got to watch as mom and dad were such great role models and friends for them. Once again, providing so many fun and valuable experiences. The support and guidance I have always had has been something I am so grateful for. It was so important as a child, trying to figure out who I was, and as an adult and parent. The love, support and opportunities throughout my life are gifts I will always be so grateful for.

From R. STEVEN HUBLER, son-in-law, husband of DeLana:

Donna has been a terrific mother-in-law and always treated me like her son. I can only recall one time she was upset with me (that I know of). I liked to tease one of our daughters, Megan, who was always happy and smiling. She was about 2 years old at the time. I would say to Megan, "She's going to crumble (cry)". Megan would say, "No!" I would reply, "Yes, she is!" The tears would start to flow. Donna didn't like that and she let me know. In my opinion, perhaps the best thing Donna did was to allow me to marry the absolutely most important person in my life, her daughter, DeLana. She has made a great life for me!

From SAMANTHA KAY HUBLER DYKES, youngest granddaughter:

I think this has taken me so long to write because I don't know where to begin. I remember growing up when asked to tell who was in your family, I would always say my mom, dad, biggest sister Ashley, middle sister Megan, Zoie, Gram, Pop, and Diane. That was always my immediate family. I always thought of us as a pack of 8 and whatever dogs we may have at the time.

Some favorite memories I have are in first grade when gram and pop surprised me, taking me to lunch. Gram makes her baked mac and cheese and walks down the backyard to eat under the tree. Sleepovers as we were younger where gram would make spaghetti and we would have bubble baths. Making a tennis ball coin holder. Going to school to see where gram taught.

As I got older, she was always at my events and soon I was having sleepovers with my high school friends. It was normal to go after school with my friends and hang out at their house. I have always thought at any point in my life that their home was an extension of mine. There are so many times I have enjoyed and cherished as an adult as well. Going to the Price is Right. Learning how to quilt with gram. Teaching in the classroom next to her as she subbed. Watching her play basketball. Seeing her be a great grandma and playing with my own kids.

I think the biggest lesson I have learned from Gram is that you can always do anything you put your mind to no matter your age. She has shown that through her many accomplishments and years of hard work. Although I wish she would take time to relax more, I have found that she truly enjoys the busyness. I look forward to many memories ahead and I am so honored to be able to spend so much time with her and have her as my grandma.

From MEGAN LEIGH HUBLER LEVENHAGEN, middle granddaughter:

Whenever I think of Gram, I think of someone who is adventurous, generous, hard-working, and selfless. I loved coming to visit the house in the country because I knew we would have some sort of adventure whether it be hunting for caterpillars on milkweed, trying to find an anthill and queen, catching frogs or picking grapes and fruit. And if we found ourselves in itch-weed, Gram would make an oatmeal bath to soothe our skin, or apply aloe straight from the plant for small cuts or sunburn. Times with Gram are always full of learning through experience and I'm thankful for everything she has taught me, things that I can now teach to Joben, Kauri, and Natalie.

Through the years she and Pop have been such a big part of my life, always supporting us at all of our activities, never missing a holiday, birthday, or any other special milestone big or small. Gram and Pop were always a team and

225

set an example for a successful relationship working together to run their home - work together to be able to have fun together once the work is done. Gram seems to have endless energy and has been involved in so many activities, and selflessly given her time and talents through volunteerism. She has touched many lives and I am proud to be her granddaughter!

From ASHLEY NICOLE HUBLER, my oldest granddaughter:

Gram, you have many amazing qualities that I admire about you - three that stand out is your desire to continually try new things, your selflessness and your love for your family.

Experiences - You always look forward to trying new activities, having new experiences, and simply doing things you haven't done before. When it comes to new experiences, you always make the most out of those experiences. Your desire to learn new things, understand other's perspectives, and continually learn is inspiring.

Selflessness - You are one of the most selfless people I know. Putting other people's feelings and preferences over your own is in your DNA. You do not complain but instead make the best out of situations and see the best in other people.

Family – Family is at the center of everything you do. The foundation you built with Pop has cascaded down multiple generations and played a huge part in shaping me into the person I am today. I always tell people I have the most awesome family and I truly mean it.

You and Diane caring for our girls for seven months during the pandemic was not convenient since you live over two hours away and likely wasn't easy (though you would never admit it), however it was such a blessing for me and special gift for the girls to get to know you so well.

In your true *selfless* nature, I know you would do absolutely anything for any one of us. And, I have so many special memories of *experiences* together.

You have helped instill in me a curiosity for new experiences, belief in myself that I can accomplish anything I set out to do, and a great appreciation for family. For that and much more, I am grateful and so thankful that you are such a large part of my life. I love you.

Great Granddaughter, Avery Leigh's note:
What's your favorite book to read with Gram? Poke-it book
What do you feel about Gram? Wonderful.
What's your favorite thing to do with Gram? Playing with her.
What's your favorite thing to play with her? Sand and play-dough.

Great Granddaughter, Logan Kay's note (My little pickle):
What do you feel about Gram? Excited.
What's your favorite thing to do with Gram? Playing with her. Doing puzzles and reading books.
What's your favorite thing to play with her? Pop-up book, puzzles and play dough.

Schuessler Family Tree

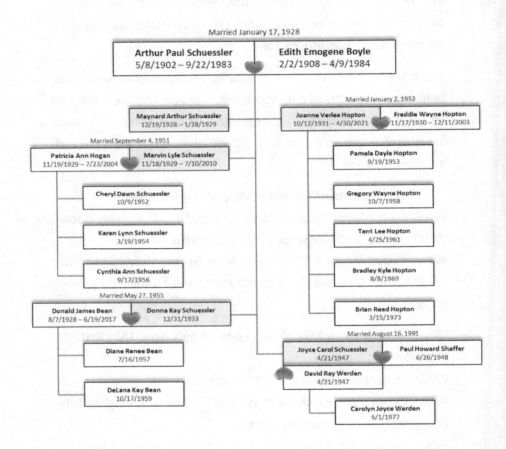

Married January 17, 1928

Arthur Paul Schuessler
5/8/1902 – 9/22/1983

Edith Emogene Boyle
2/2/1908 – 4/9/1984

Maynard Arthur Schuessler
12/19/1928 – 1/28/1929

Married January 2, 1953

Joanne Verlee Hopton
10/12/1931 – 4/30/2021

Freddie Wayne Hopton
11/17/1930 – 12/11/2003

Married September 4, 1951

Patricia Ann Hogan
11/19/1929 – 7/23/2004

Marvin Lyle Schuessler
11/18/1929 – 7/10/2010

Pamela Dayle Hopton
9/19/1953

Cheryl Dawn Schuessler
10/9/1952

Gregory Wayne Hopton
10/7/1958

Karen Lynn Schuessler
3/19/1954

Terri Lee Hopton
4/25/1961

Cynthia Ann Schuessler
9/17/1956

Bradley Kyle Hopton
8/8/1969

Married May 27, 1955

Donald James Bean
8/7/1928 – 6/19/2017

Donna Kay Schuessler
12/31/1933

Brian Reed Hopton
3/15/1973

Married August 16, 1991

Diane Renee Bean
7/16/1957

Joyce Carol Schuessler
4/21/1947

Paul Howard Shaffer
6/26/1948

David Ray Werden
4/21/1947

DeLana Kay Bean
10/17/1959

Carolyn Joyce Werden
6/1/1977

Bean Family Tree

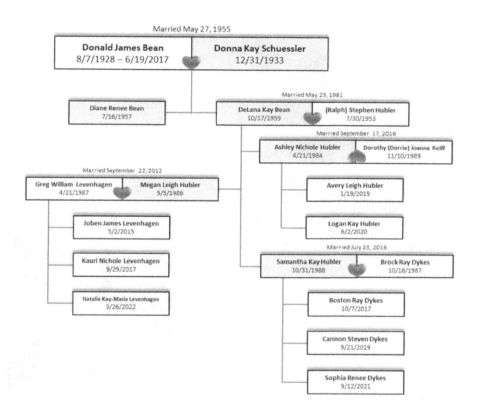

Married May 27, 1955

| Donald James Bean | Donna Kay Schuessler |
| 8/7/1928 – 6/19/2017 | 12/31/1933 |

Diane Renee Bean	Married May 23, 1981
7/16/1957	DeLana Kay Bean / (Ralph) Stephen Hubler
	10/17/1959 / 7/30/1953

Married September 17, 2016

| Ashley Nichole Hubler | Dorothy (Dorrie) Joanna Reiff |
| 4/21/1984 | 11/10/1989 |

Married September 22, 2012

| Greg William Levenhagen | Megan Leigh Hubler |
| 4/21/1987 | 5/5/1986 |

| Avery Leigh Hubler |
| 1/19/2019 |

| Joben James Levenhagen |
| 5/2/2015 |

| Logan Kay Hubler |
| 6/2/2020 |

| Kauri Nichole Levenhagen |
| 9/29/2017 |

Married July 23, 2016

| Samantha Kay Hubler | Brock Ray Dykes |
| 10/31/1988 | 10/18/1987 |

| Natalie Kay-Marie Levenhagen |
| 3/26/2022 |

| Boston Ray Dykes |
| 10/7/2017 |

| Cannon Steven Dykes |
| 9/21/2019 |

| Sophia Renee Dykes |
| 9/12/2021 |

229

Pictures That I Had to Include
Adventures

Holding my nephew, Brian's boa constrictor!

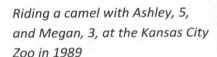

Riding a camel with Ashley, 5, and Megan, 3, at the Kansas City Zoo in 1989

Riding an elephant with Ashley and Megan at the Kansas City Zoo in 1989

<u>*More Adventures*</u>

Taking a ride on a hot air balloon with DeLana-2021

Skydiving with Samantha, Megan and DeLana-2008

Parasailing at Lahaina in Maui with Diane in 2011

Crazy Family Competitions

Everyone decorated their own Easter bonnet for a competions-2012 DeLana's won!

At Christmas, we sometimes have a Scavenger Hunt. One of the items was to wrap a person as a present.

One of the items on the list was to have the entire group jump in the air at the same time. I think Greg must be part frog!

Family Outings

Many years we took a vacation with the whole family in the summer to a Midwestern location. This picture is at the Science Museum in Kansas City.

When my granddaughters were little, they would visit their Aunt Diane in Manchester, IA. They went to the fish hatchery there, many parks (including the Coggon Clown swing) and then would come home and have a TV dinner as a treat It has continued with another generation in 2023.

Family (Joyce and Paul)

My collaborator, Joyce and her husband, Paul Shaffer-2015

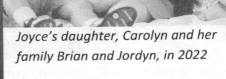

Joyce's daughter, Carolyn and her family Brian and Jordyn, in 2022

Carolyn playing the violin which she had been playing since she was 4.

Donna, Joanne, and Joyce in 2012

Family (Joanne and Rick)

Joanne and Rick

Joanne's son, Greg, who made the wonderful family trees at the end of this book and his family at Justin and Alli's wedding-2023

Most of Joanne's family in Florida in 2017

Family (Joanne and Rick)

Joanne's entire family (plus Joyce and Paul) outside her funeral in April, 2021

The last Thanksgiving visit with all of the Hopton-2004- When the kids were growing up, we went out to the Hoptons in Ohio for every Thanksgiving, right after we got out of school on Wednesday. This was the first year after Rick had died and we decided to switch it up and have everyone come to Iowa. Almost everyone stayed at our house or DeLana's house except for one family!

Family(Marvin and Pat)

Marvin and Pat's family-(from left)-Karen, Dave, Pat, Marvin, Cheryl
(holding Cynthia's baby, Stephanie), Doug and Cynthia

Marvin, Donna and Joyce in 1990

*Karen, Joyce, me,
Diane-Karen often
comes back to Iowa
to visit. She lives in
New York so when we
visit Joyce and Paul in
Connecticut, we get
to see her too!*

Family (Richard and Carol)

Carol and Richard Bean in 2001

Richard and Carol's whole family in 2022-(From left-Jeff, Genea, Andy, Carol, Alex, Angie, Steve and Courtney

Jeff's family (From left)-Jeff, Alex, Blake, Drew, Genea-2007

Family(Mary and Betty)

Betty and Mary in 1949

Then and 2018

_Aunt Elva and her children-From left-
David, Mary, David and Betty_

As children-Betty, Fred, Mary, David

Family Reunions and Friends

My Boyle cousins (From left)-Beverly and Bob Boyle, Dale Bergert, Dick Boyle, Dolores Bergert, Sharon and Merrill Boyle

I get together with my friends from high school every month.

Schuessler family reunion-1974-From left-Aunt Freida Carpenter, Diane, Millie, Marion and Kay Carpenter, Dad, DeLana, Joyce, Aunt Laura Schuessler, Mom and Me

The Favorite Quilts

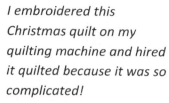

I embroidered this Christmas quilt on my quilting machine and hired it quilted because it was so complicated!

I made each of my great-grandchildren crib quilt, single bed quilt, double bed quilt and a cuddly quilt for daycare and then a queen sized quilt for each family. This is Avery's quilt-2018

This was the double bed quilt that I made for my great niece, Jordyn. It was one of the harder quilts that I made-2017

When Covid hit, I decided to take the box of quilt pieces that I had gotten from my mom and make them into quilts, table runners and centerpieces. I made 38 for my Schuessler cousins. These are a few of them.2021

Other Awards

The Linn Mar Lion Pride Award for outstanding work in our local schools. Several years I put in 700 hours!

The Ageless Hero award for community work that I had done in 1999

In 2011, I received the Lifetime Achievement Award for my work in our church.

This award from the Cedar Rapids Schools was for outstanding service to the youth of the district

242

My Most Precious Treasures

Having fun with my granddaughters, Samantha, 2, Ashley, 7 and Megan 5 in 1991

Megan and Greg's family in 2023-Joben, 8, Kauri, 5, and Natalie, 1

Samantha and Brock's family-Cannon, 4, Boston,6, and Sophia, 2, in 2023

Ashley and Dorrie's family in 2023-Avery, 5, and Logan, 3

Made in the USA
Monee, IL
01 March 2024

54216693R00134